In Order of Appearance

A parody in two acts by

Gardner McKay

SAMUEL FRENCH, INC.

Other Plays
by
Gardner McKay

MASTERS OF THE SEA

ME

SEA MARKS

TOYER

In Order of Appearance

A parody in two acts by

Gardner McKay

SAMUEL FRENCH, INC.

45 West 25th Street   7623 Sunset Boulevard
NEW YORK 10010   HOLLYWOOD 90046
LONDON   *TORONTO*

IMPORTANT BILLING AND CREDIT REQUIREMENTS

All producers of IN ORDER OF APPEARANCE *must* give credit to the Author of the Play in all programs distributed in connection with performances of the Play and in all instances in which the title of the Play appears for purposes of advertising, publicizing or otherwise exploiting the Play and/or a production. The name of the Author *must* appear on a separate line on which no other name appears, immediately following the title, and *must* appear in size of type not less than fifty percent the size of the title type.

THE PEOPLE IN THE PLAY

(not in order of appearance)

HALEN FAIRBROTHER (born TOM VICKERY), forty-five-ish. Bearish, balding, possibly bearded. A fugitive. Burdened.

MAURICE BONECREAM, older than Tom. President of Bonecream Artists Agency. Hyperactive, tyrannical, joyous, manic.

EMMA JONES FAIRBROTHER, nearly thirty. Tom's wife of nine years. Artistic. Local girl down countless generations.

ELI MORGENSTERN, mid-twenties. Hired man, lives behind Fairbrothers. Local. Slightly abstracted by a nasty fall, but subject to moments of great clarity.

DUNLOP *DUNY* SABLEHAND, late thirties. Foppish British theater agent. First-time *playwright* and plagiarist.

SHELLEY VICKERY, fifty-ish. Tom's older sister. Tall, handsome, strong-willed. Incapacitated; in wheelchair. (Shelley also appears in ACT I at age 25 without dialogue.)

Three thankless roles that can be played by one actor:

RANDALL MOSS, a private investigator.

BILLY, a limousine driver.

YO BRAVO, an ex-Desert Storm helicopter pilot.

❖ ❖ ❖ ❖ ❖

Note: *In Order of Appearance* is a sequel to Gardner McKay's earlier play *Me*, which is also available from Samuel French, Inc.

ACT I

Scene 1

(Night. The stage is black. Sound of light rain falling on roof.

A special light comes up SL or SR between proscenium and set. It focuses only on a woman facing audience, SHELLEY at her young age, a ghostly presence. She is slim, wears a long dress, her hair is down, stands looking at audience moving her eyes among them for not less than five seconds, not more than ten. Then, without moving her head, lips sealed, she smiles enigmatically at them. The special fades. She is gone.

At that instant, some where on the road outside, a car crashes. Abrupt scream of rubber tires, soft thump of car striking stump. After a moment, car door slams.

We see a light flashing through a window. A dark house, asleep. We can see a stairway rising upstage. House is small but generous. Then a rapping on a door, the sharp report of a pinky ring rather than a knuckle.

Light comes on upstairs, door opens, HALEN FAIRBROTHER appears on upstairs landing, descends, sleep-walking in long-johns, lights amber shaded lamp downstairs, opens front door wide.

Stands a well-dressed MAN from the city. Moans, enters and sits. Distinguished. He is bleeding slightly from the forehead.

Dimly seen: living room and part of kitchen. Raw wood in sight. Oilcloth kitchen table. Rain drips precisely into two buckets.

The men barely speak. HALEN wets the corner of a kitchen towel and

5

wipes the blood off the man's forehead, pronounces it non-threatening.)

VISITOR. Ugh. Oh. Ugh.

HALEN. You okay otherwise?

VISITOR. Yeah, I'm okay, I'm worried about my car.

HALEN. What's wrong with it?

VISITOR. It's a German car.

HALEN. *(Relieved.)* Could have been a Chevy. Want my wife to look at her?

VISITOR. Your wife? Why?

HALEN. She knows about cars.

VISITOR. Oh. Let's not bother her. Is there an Auto Club?

HALEN. Auto Club? Wouldn't bother them neither, nearest branch is over to Lewis.

(VISITOR looks around, feels he's with the chief of a Jivaro village.)

VISITOR. So.

HALEN. Or we could get Eli Morgenstern to fix her up. You're lucky 'cause he's only to Wadawanuck playing poker to Ted Small's.

VISITOR. Wadawanuck?

HALEN. You were just *in* Wadawanuck.

VISITOR. Oh, that. *(To himself:)* Wadawanuck.

(HALEN dials four numbers methodically on the wall phone by the kitchen.)

VISITOR. That's only four numbers.

HALEN. Yup.

VISITOR. You don't need more numbers?

HALEN. Nope. Not enough phones around here, dialin's a waste of finger time. *(Into phone.)* Ted, Halen, fellow from New York broke down his car, Eli there? *(Listens.)* No, not so bad, German car. *(Listens, laughs.)* Yup, s'what I told him. *(Listens.)* Yup.

(HALEN hangs up. Not fully awake, starts trudging upstairs.)

VISITOR. What?

HALEN. Eli lost twenty dollars.

VISITOR. Oh.

HALEN. He'll be here pretty soon more or less.

VISITOR. *(Uncertain.)* And ...?

HALEN. Well, he'll fix her up. He won't ask you for money, so could you kindly give him some to make up for his poker losses?

VISITOR. *(Nods.)* It's Eli.

HALEN. Yup. Eli Morgenstern. He's my hired hand but he's not one hundred percent since he took that nasty fall.

VISITOR. Well, you've been most kind, Mr. ...

HALEN. Halen Fairbrother.

VISITOR. *(Buttons coat.)* I'm Randall Moss. *(Indicates front door.)* But the sign says Thistledome.

TOM. Name of the house.

VISITOR. Could you just jot down your name and address for me Halen? Oh. How did you know I was from New York?

HALEN. Where else could you be from, Randall?

(HALEN starts back upstairs.)

VISITOR. *(Opens front door.)* Should I wait in the car?

HALEN. Stay where you are. There's a fifty-proof cranberry cider there, clear your switches. Turn the porch light off there *(Indicates switch,)* when you go, please.

VISITOR. Thanks, Halen, thanks. Goodnight.

HALEN. Thanks for dropping by, Randall. Goodnight.

(Door closes upstairs. Alone, RANDALL looks upstairs after HALEN.

Produces a small photograph and studies it. Takes a wallet-sized telephone out of his pocket and punches in numbers.)

VISITOR. *(Into phone, whispers excitedly.)* Maurice? You awake? It's Moss. *(Listens.)* Wadawanuck, Maine. *(Listens, glances upstairs.)* It's him. Listen to me, Maurice, I found him. He changed his name, he's got a beard, but I'm sure it's him.

Scene 2

(Afternoon light, following day. Same rain, same house, same two buckets, set in new locations, catching the tick-tock drips, steady as clockwork.

Hung on the walls are GEMMA's bold tapestries-in-progress; sections of huge flowers. Seen clearly is a sign standing against a kitchen wall:

Cider Sauce Juice

FAIRBROTHER'S
CRANBERRIES

"As good as most,
better than some."

A large boyish man in his twenties, ELI MORGENSTERN, handsome in a dog-like way, healthy, local. Seems to be a deaf mute. During the scene, we hardly know he's present. ELI hears a buzzing in his ears, is sometimes unsure of his surroundings. He's curled by the fire reading the National Enquirer, *one of many.*

ELI stands, empties a rain-drip pail into sink, warms his hands at fire, sits, pulls out candy bar, methodically strips its wrapper,

carefully flattens out his gossip-fiction-weekly, falls into a deep concentration over the material.
HALEN bursts in through front door, wet, carrying two full pails of cranberries. Once at fireplace, he kicks the logs with his boot and warms himself, then he opens his waterproof coat, starts to shed wet clothes. It seems as cold inside the house as it is outside.)

HALEN. Damp.

(ELI, engrossed in his magazine, barely looks up.)

ELI. Rainy.
HALEN. Yup.
ELI. Yup.
HALEN. What d'you figure?
ELI. Good for berries.
HALEN. About the roof I mean.
ELI. It's leakin'.
HALEN. I see that, Eli, it needs patchin'.
ELI. Best to patch roofs when the sun's out.

(ELI returns to his studies. HALEN slips out of his waterproof, drops it in a pile, shakes like a dog.
He empties his pail on the kitchen table. Shiny red berries. He takes off his hat and throws it somewhere with a flourish, regards himself in small mirror over kitchen sink. Suddenly he rhapsodizes to the walls.)

HALEN. Oh, I love to grow cranberries! I love to pick 'em just after the rain when it's been coming down hard and the berries are ready to drop. That's when I got to get out there and scoop 'em up before the coons and the birds get 'em. Little critters stand around watchin' me with that ready-to-jump look, like I were stealing what's theirs. But I always scatter a few for 'em. Who knows? If I didn't, one day they could all rise up against me.

(HALEN looks upstairs, bellows.)

> HALEN. Emma! Cranberries are ripe. Startin' to drop!
> GEMMA'S VOICE. *(From below.)* Good for them, love.
> HALEN. Where are you?
> GEMMA'S VOICE. Down here.

(Sound of milling steel from basement.)

> HALEN. *(Looking at floor.)* Oh.
> GEMMA'S VOICE. Grinding the valves.
> HALEN. Good. What about the mounts?
> GEMMA'S VOICE. Mounts are fine. Front's already in and I'm happy about the other two.
> HALEN. I love you.
> GEMMA'S VOICE. What?
> HALEN. That's great, Emma, just great. *(Rinses berries in sink. Picks out a few duffs. To the walls:)* There's a woman knows when she's happy with her engine mounts. *(Continues rhapsodizing.)* Rain! Couldn't imagine a fairer way to circulate water than in rain drops. Think of it. Tiny, pear-shaped parcels, they bring all the support we all need. Oh, my God, when He gets it right, He gets it right.

(Sound of milling stops.)

> GEMMA'S VOICE. What, darling?
> HALEN. *(Shouts.)* Rain. Tiny parcels of perfection!
> GEMMA'S VOICE. Good for the berries.

(HALEN is about to confess his love, but the milling resumes. Turns

back to mirror.)

HALEN. As for me, I can now be described as balding. Nature is giving it to me in small doses, a slow progression, careful never to startle me.

(GEMMA FAIRBROTHER appears at the back door holding an aluminum cylinder head in one hand a rag in the other. Grease on her hands and face. She is almost thirty, lovely, vibrant. Earthy. She holds the shiny cylinder high, like the Statue of Liberty, too feminine for the job.)

GEMMA. Dirt must've snuck in here.
HALEN. I never get used to you, Em.

(She goes to him. After an intimate groping ritual, they kiss, enjoying each other. An easy permanence felt between man and woman, without routine.)

GEMMA. You're wet as a bear. *(They break, give each other a high five. She glances at the cranberries.)* Oh, my God, Hale, aren't they beautiful, big as cherries!

(ELI looks up.)

ELI. H'lo, Mrs. Fairbrother.
GEMMA. Hello, Eli, rainy, huh?

(GEMMA indicates drip buckets.)

ELI. Have not your roof to patch when it begins to rain.
HALEN. That's a good one, Eli.
ELI. Those are new holes.
HALEN. When the sun comes out, right Eli?

ELI. Yup.

(No one seems to mind very much.)

GEMMA. You eating with us, Eli?
ELI. Yup.
GEMMA. There's a slab of meatloaf has your name on it, Eli.
ELI. It does?
GEMMA. Would you set the table, please?

(Rooster crows protectively, indicating trespasser.
GEMMA goes upstairs to bathe for dinner. ELI methodically begins
to set kitchen table.
TAPPING on kitchen window.)

MALE VOICE. Hello?
HALEN. *(Receptive.)* Yes?
MALE VOICE. Hello in there!
HALEN. *(Sees a stranger.)* Come around front.

(HALEN opens front door. MAURICE BONECREAM, a pale man,
bursts in. A city man dressed for the country in English
waterproofs, excellent tweeds, and on his head a soft Borsalino.
MAURICE speaks in fast flourishes. He wears more than one
gold accessory. He assumes he's alone in the house with HALEN
until ELI eventually stirs.)

MAURICE. Gotcha.
HALEN. Excuse me?
MAURICE. Gotcha. *(Less certainly.)* Tom?
HALEN. No, it isn't.
MAURICE. It's not? *(Renewed conviction.)* It is. It is you.
    HALEN. Yes, it is me, but it's not Tom. It's someone else.
(Patiently.) Now, who are you?

MAURICE. Tom Vickery?

(HALEN extends his hand, to calm the lunatic.)

HALEN. I'm Halen Fairbrother.
MAURICE. No, no, I'm not Tom Vickery, you are.
HALEN. I'm another person. I'm Halen Fairbrother.
MAURICE. Good name.
HALEN. Yes, it is.
MAURICE. But you're not him, you're Tom Vickery.
HALEN. Who are you?
MAURICE. Maurice Bonecream.
HALEN. Good name. *(They regard each other. No one moves.)* You must be lost.

MAURICE. I am not lost. I am Maurice Bonecream, you know me.

HALEN. I don't know you.

MAURICE. Yes, you do. It's been nineteen years. Nineteen good years. Maurice, your beloved agent. How could you forget?

HALEN. *(Bewildered.)* Why would I not be who I say I am?

MAURICE. Many, many reasons, Tom, six million of them.

HALEN. *(Recovering, in a Maine accent.)* Someone must be Tom Vickery, somewhere else, not around here. You're a city boy. Why don't you go back down to the city? This is Maine.

MAURICE. I can forget a name, a face, even a deal, but not how someone talks. You're not dead, Tom! Oh, God, Tom, it's you, alive, in hiding all these years.

(MAURICE is crying, currying, wagging his tail. He is too happy for what is to be seen. He attempts to kiss him. HALEN shoves him away.)

HALEN. Go away, whoever you are. I don't know what you're talking about. Get out or we'll haul you out and drop you in a ditch.

MAURICE. For what? For finding my long lost client and bringing him the best news of his life? A ditch? *(Pause.)* Okay, I'll play. Maurice Bonecream, your literary agent, until you died in a crash nineteen years ago. *(MAURICE sits, overcome. To him, HALEN is TOM.)* It is you under that beard, isn't it? *(MAURICE fishes out two scraps of paper, compares them. One is the scrap HALEN wrote out for RANDALL.)* This is your handwriting. It matches your suicide note.

(HALEN is TOM and they are both trapped. TOM dissolves slightly. Surrenders.)

TOM. *(Nods, quietly.)* How'd you do it?
MAURICE. Remember Randall Moss the other night? He worked for me.
TOM. Doing what?
MAURICE. Finding you. He did, so he's out of a job.
TOM. How?
MAURICE. If you die, Tom, you automatically give up your right to apply for a new driver's license. *(MAURICE produces two licenses.)* Two licenses, two names. One face. *(Eyes licenses.)* Why are you smiling on the new one?
TOM. I was happy then.

(MAURICE stares at TOM, wells up again.)

MAURICE. It's a miracle.
TOM. No miracle.
MAURICE. *(Glances around.)* Nineteen years.
TOM. Where does the time go?
MAURICE. You'd never drive off a cliff, Tom, it's a cheap plot. *(Sobs again, recovers.)* I love the beard by the way, hang onto that. Hey, you're balding. Look, me too!

(MAURICE raises his Borsalino.)

TOM. I always wondered; maybe he'll turn up one day. Here you are. *(Resigned.)* I've had some glory seasons. That's enough for any man. *(Evenly.)* What do you want?

MAURICE. You hurt me, Tom, a long time ago. Setting fire to me was a heartless, heartless act.

TOM. I set fire to your office.

MAURICE. And me, I was in it.

TOM. I wanted to destroy it and everything in it. Okay, and you. It was wrong. Still it was too good for you.

MAURICE. You could be right, I wasn't always Mr. Niceguy in those days. But burning someone to death? Primitive, Tom, no one's done that since .... medieval Spain. Are you Catholic?

(TOM shushes him, points to bedroom door upstairs.)

TOM. You sued me for six million dollars.

MAURICE. I was hurt.

TOM. We can settle this out of court. *(Sweeps hand around room.)* Take what you want.

(MAURICE briefly surveys the junk with distaste.)

MAURICE. I don't need any more buckets.

TOM. I can pay you the rest. Six million at ten percent for twenty years, that's — twelve million, plus the original six million, plus expenses. Let's call it twenty million. In twelve hundred years I'll be caught and paying only ten times that annually for interest.

MAURICE. Like the national debt.

TOM. It's why you're here, isn't it?

MAURICE. Oh, Tom, that was then, this is now. I don't want your money. *(Laughs gaily.)* I'm dropping all charges.

(MAURICE tries to embrace TOM. TOM stiffens.)

TOM. *(Surprised.)* I don't know what to say. *(Suspiciously.)* You did not spend a year tracking me down me to tell me that.

MAURICE. Yes. Well, not entirely. Listen. Remember the good old days?

TOM. What good old days? You never took my calls. You didn't even have hold music, you had hold commercials.

MAURICE. Just a novelty. I want to ask you something. Hint: Remember your play about a crazy family?

TOM. My play about a crazy family.

MAURICE. Off-beat comedy cum tragic love story?

TOM. Right.

MAURICE. *(Prompting him.)* The spin was, the kid's pretending to be retarded, but all the while he's sleeping with his big sister.

TOM. I remember, I remember. My only play.

MAURICE. You have a great serio-comic tragic flair, my friend.

TOM. That play was the reason I tried to kill you.

MAURICE. Yes, yes, what did you call it?

TOM. *Autopsy of Love.*

MAURICE. *Autopsy of Love.* How could I forget that title?

TOM. Because you told me it was unproduceable.

MAURICE. That's her.

TOM. You lied. You told me you'd submitted it to twenty-three Broadway producers and that they all turned it down. No one ever saw it. You threw it away. Right?

MAURICE. I misplaced it. I only had one copy.

TOM. You were ashamed of it.

MAURICE. *(Protectively.)* I saved you, Tom; the critics would have pecked your eyes out and dined on your flesh. *(Holds hand up.)* Don't talk, listen, I bring you good news. The deal of a lifetime.

TOM. The critics are hungry . .

MAURICE. Listen to me. *(MAURICE waves for silence. Waxes.)* I'm on the West End. It's wet, like this. My collar is up. I'm dressed entirely in Polo. I'm walking the night searching for product. With great difficulty I have obtained a single balcony ticket to the hit off-beat-comedy-love-story called *Tomby*. It's been running on the West End for two years. Big hit. Single balcony seat from a scalper who looked like — who is it? — Oliver Twist. I'm sitting there in the balcony watching this ... this controversial comedy about ....

TOM. West End Avenue?

MAURICE. What West End Avenue? Where have you been?

TOM. Wadawanuck.

MAURICE. The West End. London. London's West End. I have a branch there. Will you shut up? *(Waxes on.)* I'm sitting high in the balcony, I can barely see the stage so I'm listening. It dawns on me, something familiar's going on down there, very *deja vu*, my memory reaches way back, twenty years, suddenly it speaks to me. It says, "you're watching *Autopsy of a Love*. Your *wonderful* play, word for word. I'm in shock. I'm helpless. What can I do?

TOM. Can I know what we're talking about?

MAURICE. Watch me. Look at my face. I'm smiling. Watch my mouth move. Your play: London, your play is running in. A very big hit: Two years. A seat you cannot get.

TOM. What are you trying to say?

MAURICE. Is there no oxygen in Maine? Your play, *Autopsy of Love* is now called *Tomby*. Your play: Crazy Tomby, his nun-like older sister, consenting adult incest. Plus jealous boyfriend, meddling mom, dopey dad, the full boat. Your play has been running in London and is opening on Broadway next week. You are about to become a surprise Broadway playwright this season without lifting a finger.

(ELI moves. MAURICE notices him, leaps away.)

MAURICE. Jesus, who's that?

TOM. This is Eli Morgenstern. Maurice Bonecream.

(ELI looks up, nods, continues reading.)

MAURICE. He's been here the whole time? Maybe he

understands.

    TOM. Eli doesn't "hear" very well, do you Eli?

    ELI. Yup, like Beethoven.

(MAURICE looks to TOM inquiringly. TOM nods. ELI's not 100%.)

    TOM. *(Quietly.)* He works here.

(ELI pours himself cranberry cider. Curls up again by the hearth to study the National Enquirer.*)*

    MAURICE. Uh, so, two years on the West End. Already your play's made a fortune.

    TOM. I guess that's good news.

    MAURICE. I guess it is, Tom. Never mind what it'll earn touring Toronto, Sydney, Chicago, Paris, Berlin, San Francisco, Tokyo ... it's big, and getting bigger. Cheer up.

(MAURICE sits, overcome by the excitement.)

    TOM. So, you brought me a check.

    MAURICE. There's a snag we're facing here. Someone else put his name on your play.

    TOM. Someone else?

    MAURICE. Someone entirely different from you says he wrote your play. A new person.

    TOM. Who wrote it this time?

    MAURICE. An Englishman. An imposter, a plagiarist. A mountebank. Young. Wears tanning cosmetics. Full head of hair.

    TOM. How did he get his hands on it?

    MAURICE. He used to work for me in the mailroom. Just a kid. He took it home....

    TOM. You gave it to him?

    MAURICE. No! When I put your play aside, he must have stolen it.

TOM. From a wastebasket.

MAURICE. I never trusted that little shit. He must have known you were dead.

TOM. Is this his first play?

MAURICE. According to his publicist, it is.

TOM. My first, too.

MAURICE. And your most abnormal. You were too far ahead of your time, Tom. I always told you; base your work on a recent hit and use it as your starting point.

TOM. That was always very bad advice, Maurice.

MAURICE. You want to stay a little bit ahead of your time, Tom, not a whole lot.

TOM. Right. If you're one inch ahead of your time, you're a genius. If you're a foot ahead, you're a lunatic.

(Suddenly ELI looks up from his text.)

ELI. Mr. Fairbrother, lobster blood is pale blue.

(A startled silence.)

TOM . You knew that, didn't you, Eli?

ELI. No, I didn't know that.

MAURICE. I didn't know that either.

TOM. Well, it is, even if it says it in the *Enquirer*.

(MAURICE becomes slightly exasperated.)

MAURICE. He changed your lovely title to *Tomby*. You're being very calm about this.

TOM. I am. I like that title better. And what's the new author's name?

MAURICE. Dunlop Sablehand.

TOM. No one is called Dunlop Sablehand.

MAURICE. He is. We used to call him Duny *(say: Doony)* at the office. When he left me, he became an agent on his own in London.

TOM. I believe I'm going to be sick.

MAURICE. Don't bash agents. We do some good in the world. *(Thinks.)* He got your play to Broadway.

TOM. True.

MAURICE. They could all take lessons from you today, believe me.

TOM. So long ago. I had fierce anger then, I was so young, I believed in the almighty power of love, and I trusted.
Then I learned to be comfortable with despair.

MAURICE. You were my boy genius, I knew it then, I know it now.

TOM. Let's try to stick to the truth, Maurice, collect your thoughts. Why did you come here?

MAURICE. *(Gushing.)* I love you. *(Recovers.)* Hey, this Sablehand's already getting a serious reputation based on your play, he's becoming a discussed playwright. You don't seem to care.

TOM. I suppose you're doing something about it.

MAURICE. This is me, here, doing it. I'd take him to court, but I don't have a scrap of evidence says you wrote it, the court throws it out. They wouldn't give me credibility.

TOM. I wonder why.

MAURICE. Tom, please, this court is in London. It's not normal. Wigs.

TOM. I gave you my carbon copy, I kept the original.

MAURICE. *(Trembling.)* I want that original, Tom.

TOM. *(Shushes him.)* Will you stop calling me Tom? Tom is dead. I am Halen. My wife doesn't know any Toms.

MAURICE. *(Relieved.)* You're married! She'll be happy to see me. You don't really want me to go along with this Tom-is-dead crap, do you? C'mon, cheer up, make an effective comeback.

TOM. A comeback from the grave would be an effective comeback. I can see the cover of *People Magazine*, screaming

"Resurrection!"

MAURICE. *(Overwhelmed.)* Oh, God, yes, *People Magazine*.

TOM. Stop it, Maurice. I'm not going to be part of this. I'm not coming back from the dead, understand?

MAURICE. Come back to New York instead, covered in glory, they won't know the difference. Get real.

TOM. New York is not real.

MAURICE. This is real: I can sell your play to the movies, easy. *(To ELI.)* Tell me why I bothered to bring him the most magnificent news he's ever gotten in his entire life?

(ELI doesn't notice.)

TOM . I'm just not coming back from the dead for you. We're okay here. We don't need you. Thank you.

MAURICE. Oh, that's fine, kill the messenger. You don't need to hide anymore. Here I am. Try to consider: Don't you want to nail someone who's stolen untold millions from you.

TOM. *(Realizing.)* What is ten percent of untold millions?

MAURICE. *(Wounded.)* Please, Tom, this not about my ten percent, this is about revenge.

TOM. I've always been moved by your personal interest, but hunting me down in the Maine woods for your ten percent is .... *(Sudden disbelief.)* We still have a contract, don't we?

(MAURICE unfolds a letter of agreement.)

MAURICE. *(Warmly.)* Lifetime.

TOM. Like herpes.

MAURICE. You must honor it, Tom. *(Rhetorically.)* Is that your signature?

TOM. I'm legally dead.

(He hands TOM the paper, typed on both sides.)

MAURICE. *(Gravely.)* But I'm not. My lawsuit is still on the calendar. I don't want to take you to court, but I'm entitled to something. That's only fair.

TOM. *(Reads.)* ... ten percent paid to you by me or my heirs, survivors, next-of-kin, their friends, grandchildren ... in perpetuity ... all writings, thoughts, ideas .... Nineteen years ago March. I had hair, dreams. My wife was eight.

(TOM balls it up and throws it toward the fireplace, misses.)

MAURICE. It's a copy. *(Sighs.)* You should be happier about this than you are. I worry about you.

TOM. *(Politely.)* What would it take to make you go away and pretend that you were never here?

MAURICE. What are you hiding from? *(Answering.)* Okay. All I need is your original copy of *Autopsy of Love* to take Sablehand to court.

TOM. I don't have it.

MAURICE. I need it. Promise I'll only make you rich and never bother you again.

TOM. Why would I keep it? Unanimously rejected as it was by twenty-three Broadway producers?

MAURICE. I know it's in a trunk. Every writer has an old trunk. *(Prompts.)* And it's always covered with European hotel labels.

TOM. No old trunk.

MAURICE. I want to show the world I was always right about you.

TOM. Excuse me?

MAURICE. I didn't believe in you?

TOM. Jesus, Maurice.

MAURICE. Okay, okay, maybe I halfway believed in you then, but I believe one hundred percent in you now, and without your original copy, how can we prove Sablehand's lying?

TOM. I guess we can't.

MAURICE. We keep going 'round and 'round here, Tom, I don't

want to sue you, do I? Find the manuscript.

TOM. Then we'll be even?

MAURICE. *(Hand to God.)* So be it.

(MAURICE produces SABLEHAND's twenty-page contract.)

TOM. More contracts?

MAURICE. Sablehand's. Look at this scum, how dare he? *(Reads.)* "... this play, *Tomby*, is original and has not been copied from any other work ...." Signed Dunlop Sablehand.

TOM. Even you wouldn't do that.

MAURICE. *(Folds contract.)* He's a dead bunny. He signed a half-million-dollar deal for film rights. Zilch. I'll get double that when it gets to Broadway. I can triple that in Hollywood.

TOM. You've been to Hollywood?

MAURICE. Been to Hollywood? I am Hollywood. I have a branch of Bonecream Artists Agency in Beverly Hills. When I set this deal I'll fly you out for lunch.

TOM. Doesn't it ever feel funny, being an agent? I'm curious; what does it really feel like? No offense, but having no talent of your own? You don't build, you don't grow, you don't create. Isn't it like living off other people's blood? Dark red rubber tubes flowing from their arms into yours?

MAURICE. You're still angry at me, Tom I can tell. *(Pauses.)* Why don't we take a break? I brought a couple of bottles of Echezeaux '85. Shall I have my driver bring 'em in?

(Waits a moment while TOM settles.)

TOM. Go ahead.

(MAURICE opens a wallet-sized phone.)

MAURICE. *(Into phone.)* Billy, bring me the wooden box in the back of the car.

(MAURICE folds the tiny micro-pocket-voice into his pocket.)

ELI. Those tiny devices are called progress, aren't they? Tribal man used rocks to defend his necessities, now he goes to war to defend his luxuries.

(MAURICE, barely aware of ELI's ramblings, looks around for glasses.)

MAURICE. Glasses? *(TOM waves toward kitchen. MAURICE opens a kitchen cabinet, an object falls out. MAURICE picks up a dark sponge, rolls his eyes. Looks around.)* You're poor, Tom, I can tell. *(There's a knock at the front door.)* Possibly broke. *(Answers knock.)* Yes, Billy. *(The front door opens and a chauffeur enters carrying a wooden box: a case of wine.)* Please open one.
BILLY. Yes, Mr. Bonecream.

(BILLY uses Swiss Army knife to pry open case. MAURICE studies the rustic cottage with distaste.)

MAURICE. You get a good break on the rent up here, huh?
TOM. I don't rent it, I own it.
MAURICE. *(Incredulous.)* You bought this. *(MAURICE assesses the glassware, glances around. Reminiscing.)* I was poor once. Arrived in Monaco luggage lost, begged for my supper from a tall lady who pressed a 100-franc chip in my hand and sat me down at the baccarat table. By dawn I owned a small Greek restaurant. Feta cheese, calamari. La! It makes no sense, does it? *(BILLY withdraws cork with Swiss Army corkscrew. MAURICE indicates dismissal.)* Thanks, Billy. *(BILLY exits. MAURICE holds up a tumbler.)* Where does the time go? Glasses?
TOM. Use that other one in the sink. *(MAURICE does and pours*

red wine into tumbler. They half-toast, drink.) How'd you even conceive of looking for me?

MAURICE. I was suspicious from the start, Tom, it smelled like a typical writer's plot. Even your obituary read like a movie-of-the-week: "On the French Riviera, a Tom Vickery was killed when his Daimler flew off the serpentine corniche into the Mediterranean." Well, you were never found but small body parts later identified as calf's liver and flank steak were washed up along with your New York Knicks jacket. A Daimler?

TOM. Stolen. So, how'd you get from there to here?

MAURICE. *(Nods.)* Well, I only got interested last year when I saw your play in London, right? I got your fingerprints from your arson-murder arraignment. An ex-cop matched them to state drivers' licenses. I started in Hawaii. Maine is last state I looked.

TOM. That's why I'm here.

MAURICE. Well, anyway, you can return a success.

TOM. I don't think I can, Maurice.

MAURICE. How can you not come back?

TOM. Why?

MAURICE. Riches? You're poor, Tom, is that being unfair?

TOM. I'm a farmer, now. I'm developing a cranberry wine. Try some?

(He pours. MAURICE raises his hand palm out: No.)

MAURICE. This is not a normal response.

TOM. Oh, I'm sure but that the woman wouldn't mind a better car and I guess I wouldn't mind a wine cellar stocked with Echezeaux, but for now I'll settle for my fermented berries. We live in acceptable poverty. I don't want the subdued respect of strangers. The I.R.S. ignores me. No, I refuse to come back from the dead, think of the paperwork. Go away.

MAURICE. I wasn't asking you to appear on Good Morning America, only in court where you'll swear you wrote *Tomby.* One little day in court.

TOM. In England. My wife doesn't know about any of this. She's a lovely woman, she sews tapestries, aren't they beautiful? She sells them at the summer fairs. She wants to run for mayor of Wadawanuck. She's the difference between a flower in a field and a flower in a vase. A brilliant woman and I'm very much in love with her. I couldn't be happier. You're rocking our boat, Bonecream.

MAURICE. You're rejecting me to protect this infant who sews tapestries and keeps you clean? This is Maurice. You want me to believe you'd deny yourself a fortune for clean living? It never happened.

TOM. What do I need with you?

MAURICE. You're standing on your dick, Tom.

TOM. Well, at least I'm able to.

(As if on cue, silently GEMMA appears at the head of the stairs fresh from the bath and dressed in a fetching housedress. She is eavesdropping.)

MAURICE. If you're worried about your transgressions, arson, attempted murder, fake driver's license, false tax returns, I can go either way. My lawyer's from the firm that got Nixon off. What are you really hiding from?

TOM. Nothing! I'm happy. We value our meals, we sip, we don't gulp, we taste, we don't eat when we're not hungry. Kippers on Sunday. Smell the rosemary bread? We savor, we listen to music, the rain.

MAURICE. You're serious.

TOM. Okay. I did wrong, but I felt I had to set fire to you.

MAURICE. And you left a legacy I'm trying to erase but before I take you to court, let me talk to your wife, she sounds sensible. I'll be gentle.

(GEMMA has hardly breathed.)

TOM. No, you won't. You're a bad dream, Maurice, go away.

MAURICE. Why would I go away? With that old manuscript, yes. Now, don't make me tell her all that other bad stuff. You're still crazy, aren't you, Tom?

TOM. Am I? This is nothing. You ought to see me under a full moon.

(GEMMA, now irresistibly fascinated, descends the stairs. ELI looks up, notices her. TOM realizes they've been overheard.)

ELI. Hello, Mrs. Fairbrother.

GEMMA. Hello, Eli. Thanks for setting the table. *(To MAURICE.)* Who are you?

MAURICE. Let me take that one. You must be Emma.

GEMMA. Gemma. He calls me Emma, I'm not sure why, my name's Gemma.

MAURICE. Gemma, may I? I was just now telling your husband that I cannot understand why he wants to hide up here in the wilderness watching the grass grow.

GEMMA. That's one of our favorite things to do! When it's spring, sometimes we fall asleep lying out in the sun reading aloud, near the new grass. Suddenly I'll wake up just as a tiny shoot breaks through the earth, I can almost hear it pushing up, it's very pale, not yet green ....

TOM. And slower. Than the moonrise.

MAURICE. *(Troubled.)* Hmmm, I never stopped and .... That's very ... nice.

TOM. The ultimate nonverbal communication.

GEMMA. Or summer at noon: the sound of a push lawnmower in the distance.

TOM. The aroma of the new-cut grass on the green summer wind.

MAURICE. Alright, alright, I should have said ... hiding up here watching paint dry.

ELI. *(Looks up.)* Watching paint dry is great. At first it's real shiny ....

MAURICE. Stop!

TOM. See? It's a permanent carnival up here. We never close.

GEMMA. *(To MAURICE.)* Are you staying to dinner?

MAURICE. Well, I don't know. Am I staying to dinner, Tom?

GEMMA. Who's Tom?

MAURICE. *(Delighted.)* He is.

(TOM sits, crushed, head in hands.)

TOM. I'm Tom.

GEMMA. This is a joke.

MAURICE. No, Gemma, your husband Tom is that rarest of all endangered species. The American playwright in his natural setting, about to make love to Broadway.

GEMMA. What's he saying, Hale?

TOM. He's telling you that when I came into Wadawanuck town and swept you away from the accessory counter at Kraus', and told you I was a cranberry grower, I was exaggerating.

MAURICE. And all he was was a great American playwright.

GEMMA. *(In shock.)* That's fascinating.

TOM. It's not fascinating. I only wrote one play.

GEMMA. Oh, Hale, how wonderful! You're a has-been.

TOM. A have been.

GEMMA. Well, better to have-been one than to might-have-been a never-was one.

MAURICE. A one who is about to become rich and famous.

GEMMA. *(To MAURICE.)* Who are you, really?

MAURICE. Excuse me, he's being rude, I am Maurice Bonecream, your husband's longtime agent and friend, if I may call you Gemma, what a lovely name, I have been tirelessly searching for him to inform him and now you of your spectacular good fortune.

GEMMA. What a kind man.

MAURICE. I've always been here for him.

GEMMA. Why are you being so rude to him, Hale?

TOM. Tom. I'm not Hale.

MAURICE. I can see this is quite a day for you.

GEMMA. *(Hurt.)* There is no ... Halen Fairbrother?

TOM. Maybe once, I found the name in the Old Graveyard.

GEMMA. That's why it sounded familiar.

TOM. Gemma's folks been here eight generations.

GEMMA. What's your last name?

TOM. Vickery.

GEMMA. *(Distastefully.)* I guess that makes me Gemma Vickery. Why didn't you ever tell me? What'll the neighbors call me?

MAURICE. Mrs. Vickery when they find out how many millions you're worth, including foreign royalties and movie rights.

GEMMA. A lot's going on here and I feel very left out. Now, you've suddenly appeared out of Hale's past.

MAURICE. Yes, I ....

GEMMA. And you said you were going to make us rich.

MAURICE. If he'll only agree to my simple request. All I want him to do is find his lost manuscript so I can turn it into millions. Without it ... grief. I'm appealing to you, Gemma, talk sense to the man.

GEMMA. What manuscript? Will you slow down? How would you like to find out you've been married to two men for nine years?

MAURICE. Let me field that one. I'd say no problemo, Gemma, you get a new man and you get to keep the old one. And you'll be damned if you'll just sit there and be made rich without knowing why.

TOM. Why do we need more money?

GEMMA. More than what?

MAURICE. That's suspicious. Listen to yourself, Tom, that's like asking, why do I need more time?

TOM. No, money can't buy time.

MAURICE. Well, time can't buy money, Tom, look around you. *(Favoring GEMMA.)* Chateau Echezaux ... Cartier ... Chanel ... Harry

Winston ... Luis Vuitton ....

TOM. She's not a materialist like you, Maurice.

GEMMA. Let him finish.

MAURICE. Cairo ... Testarosa ... sybaritic baths ... foot massages, pedicures, oil scented facials, hair treatments every morning.

TOM. Who are you, Satan?

MAURICE. Oh, come on, Tom ....

GEMMA. I'm listening.

MAURICE. What about travel? When was the last time you flew to Paris?

GEMMA. What about Boston?

MAURICE. What about shopping for shoes in New York?

GEMMA. What about shopping for shoes in Wadawanuck?

TOM. Simplify, simplify.

GEMMA. Yes, love, we've done that for nine years, maybe now let's do something else.

MAURICE. Yeah, how'd you get this way, Tom?

TOM. Money is complicated, Emma.

MAURICE. How would you know?

GEMMA. Oh, let's have some nice money, darling, you've worked hard.

TOM. Growing cranberries, outwitting the weather.

MAURICE. See what I mean? What's he hiding from, Gemma? Look at me; I'm a simple, very rich man ... *(Grasping an example.)* these are six-hundred-dollar-shoes.

TOM. Then you won't mind walking me out to the bog for a few buckets of berries.

MAURICE. Are you crazy? These shoes are not for harvesting fruit, they're for meetings.

GEMMA. Stop being so rude. Yes, Maurice, we're very interested in finding whatever it is you're looking for, aren't we, Hale? Now what was all that about ... a lawsuit?

MAURICE. *(Dismissing it.)* Oh, I once sued your husband for six million.

GEMMA. Six million dollars?

MAURICE. It sounds like more than it is, Gemma.

GEMMA. It does? Are you still suing him?

MAURICE. Only if he refuses to give me his lost play.

(ELI looks up from his reading.)

ELI. Mrs. Fairbrother?

GEMMA. *(Too loudly.)* Yes, Eli. *(Calmly.)* Yes, Eli.

ELI. Here's this man built a piano that couldn't play Mozart.

TOM. About time.

GEMMA. Is that what it says? *(ELI nods.)* I can believe that.

MAURICE. I find that very hard to believe.

ELI. Definitely *commedia dell' arte*.

MAURICE. Where did you learn to say *commedia dell' arte*, young man? *(ELI reads, oblivious.)* Where did he learn to say those words? Who is he?

TOM. Eli studied at the Yale Drama School.

MAURICE. Seriously.

GEMMA. Before his fall.

TOM. He fell from the roof.

GEMMA. His mind was elsewhere. He thought he was downstairs.

ELI. I never did want to be anything but a roofer.

(MAURICE eyes the dripping roof.)

GEMMA. *(Grumbling.)* Gemma Vickery? Does it have to be me?

MAURICE. I love that name, I don't know why.

TOM. I need a smoke. *(TOM pulls out a cigar. Goes to kitchen door.)* I smoke in the henhouse. I got a rooster likes cigar smoke.

GEMMA. *(Whimsically.)* It spoils my silk drapes.

TOM. *(To MAURICE.)* Try my cranberry wine over there.

Organically fermented, 60-proof, works like antifreeze.

 MAURICE. But I don't drink ....

 TOM. You should, Maurice.

(TOM exits out kitchen door. MAURICE listens. After a moment a threatened rooster crows, indicating that TOM's lit a match near the henhouse.

ELI looks up from his studies in sadness and wonder.)

 ELI. It says here that I'll probably die never knowing how a balloon is made.

(MAURICE checks his watch.)

 MAURICE. I know I will. *(Change: serious.)* Listen, Gemma. Please. Will you hunt for the lost play? It's close, I can feel it.

 GEMMA. Yes! A play, imagine, he never told me.

 MAURICE. He spoke of it in the present tense, didn't he? Gives me hope.

 GEMMA. Stacks of old papers in the attic.

 MAURICE. Look for a beat up trunk with labels pasted on it. They all have one. You're a rich woman, Gemma, I'm sorry, he'll be rich too, whether he wants to be or not. *(MAURICE fishes out a business card.)* Here are all my numbers. Hide it, he'll tear it up. If you find the play, he'll tear that up, too, so don't tell him, tell me. It's called *Autopsy of Love*.

 GEMMA. Why was it so embarrassing to you?

 MAURICE. That's easy. *(Takes a breath.) Tomby*, Act One: Twin boys. Kids playing baseball. Greg cracks Tom with bat. Tom wakes up in hospital with a brain disorder. Sees his family hovering around him. His older sister pities him and decides to devote her life to him instead of marrying Mr. Right. Tom likes this idea, all this adoration and service from everyone. So as he slowly gets well, he keeps it a secret. Are you with me? ACT TWO: Tom still pretending brain damage but now he's sleeping with his older sister. When was the last time you saw a comedy about incest?

(TOM re-enters holding his cigar.)

TOM. *(Gravely.)* I had a thought out there; I remember now, I gave it to the paper recycler.

MAURICE. Don't joke.

TOM. Why don't you subpoena your twenty-three Broadway producers?

GEMMA. *(To TOM.)* Incest?

TOM. It's clean incest, Emma. *(GEMMA looks askance.)* Father-daughter incest is not clean. Clean is two consenting adults who are in love; who just happen to be related and wish they weren't.

MAURICE. *(Chuckles.)* You got a wicked sense of humor, my friend.

TOM. It's running in London two years.

MAURICE. I know, what can I tell you? Suddenly there's a market for smut.

TOM. Not smut, Maurice, love. It's a love story.

MAURICE. I beg your pardon, Tom, but who knew an incest-comedy-love-story would ever be a hit?

(MAURICE laughs alone. Sees it's time to go.)

TOM. *(With hostility.)* It's *go* time, Maurice.

MAURICE. Right. I'm giving you three days. *(Conspiratorially.)* It was my great pleasure meeting you at last, Gemma.

GEMMA. There's meatloaf enough for everyone.

(TOM gives them both a mean look.)

MAURICE. Perhaps next time, thank you, Gemma. Long drive. *(To TOM.)* Why don't you care what happens to your play, Tom?

That haunts me.

TOM. Finish your wine, Maurice.

MAURICE. *(Toasts them.)* To friends old and new. A friendship without wine is like ... a day without sun.

ELI. *(Looking up.)* A day without sun is like a cloudy day.

(All nod in grave assent. MAURICE gulps his wine.)

MAURICE. *(To all.)* Well, time to be heading down to the city.

TOM. Speaking of beheading; if you breathe a word of my existence ....

MAURICE. *(Gravely.)* Find me the play and I won't need to. I'll be up again Wednesday, Tom. Have a nice day.

TOM. A little too late for that, Maurice.

Scene 3

(Late the next night. The living room by candlelight. GEMMA sits on the floor, reading a worn, one-hundred page play script bound by brass buttons. The low table by the couch that's been covered by a large silk shawl is really an old trunk. It is open, the shawl is askew, the lid is up and a padlock dangles from its broken hasp.

The only light in the room is a lone candle standing on the lid of the open trunk. The name VICKERY is stenciled faintly on one side, travel stickers abound. MAURICE was right.

Barely seen at the head of the stairs, TOM has been watching GEMMA read. She stops and lights another candle to read by from the one already burning. She becomes aware of TOM with a start.)

TOM. You seem upset.

GEMMA. Yes. *(Pause.)* Don't always be telling me how I feel.

TOM. I do that don't I?

GEMMA. Yes, and you make me more upset by telling me I'm upset when I'm not upset.

TOM. I meant upset by the play.

GEMMA. It's so ... sick.

TOM. *(Tries to make her smile.)* But will it be a hit?

GEMMA. I've never been to a play, how would I know?

TOM. It's what they call a tragi-comedy.

GEMMA. Well, it's a comedy that makes me want to vomit.

TOM. That's the tragi portion.

GEMMA. I mean this little retarded boy Tomby can barely brush his teeth, his adoring family waiting on him hand and foot, he even slept with his sister, and he was only pretending to be retarded.

TOM. Look it's a play. I made it up twenty years ago.

GEMMA. But how'd you even make up such a thing?

TOM. Storytelling. What do you think of me now?

GEMMA. I'm not sure.

TOM. *(Raises right palm.)* I promise I shall never write another play.

GEMMA. Why'd you write it at all?

TOM. I was young. I wrote it out of pain. I don't need to do that anymore, Emma.

GEMMA. Why'd you call it Autopsy of Love?

TOM. I don't remember.

GEMMA. What scares me about this *(Indicates play.)* is that we could be married all these years and never know who you really were, Tom. Maybe I never knew you.

TOM. The first thing I loved about you is that you would tell the truth even when it made you look bad. If I've accomplished one thing in my life it was finding you.

GEMMA. What else are you hiding from me, Tom?

TOM. Not a damn thing.

GEMMA. What does this ending mean? QUOTE: "Shelley Tomby incriminating scene." *(She closes play — throws it?)* Shelley was real wasn't she?

(TOM speaks after some silent urging from SHELLEY.)

TOM. She was my sister. Shelley.
GEMMA. You're Tomby. *(She knows.)* God Tom, you even used your real names.

INTERMISSION

ACT II

Scene 1

(Next day, a bright winter midday. Fire in fireplace. GEMMA is alone onstage folding a tapestry from the wall into a carton. She's been crying. She seems distracted, depressed.
A suitcase stands by the front door, various cartons stand around, packed and half-packed.
Wall phone rings.)

GEMMA. Hello? *(Listens.)* Oh, Maurice! You're on your way? Yes, it's true ... Maurice? *(Listens. She hangs up phone, looks out back window to see if TOM is about. Rooster crows, then MAURICE enters at front door without knocking.)* That was quick.

MAURICE. I called from the lawn. Where did you find it? *(She points to trunk.)* Aha, I knew it, I knew it. *(Indicates upstairs. Whispers.)* Is he?

GEMMA. He slept in the henhouse.

(MAURICE opens trunk, looks around, sees half-packed boxes. GEMMA returns to folding and packing.)

MAURICE. *(Confirming it.)* You really are leaving.

GEMMA. I can't stay.

(MAURICE looks beyond her, scanning the room.)

MAURICE. Where is it?
GEMMA. Over there by the door.
MAURICE. Where? I don't see it.

(Rooster crows again.)

GEMMA. It was there.

(TOM appears at backdoor. MAURICE retreats, repositions himself. GEMMA folds and packs, head averted from them as if she's not there.)

TOM. Hello, Maurice, is this a happy coincidence, or were you drawn here by the scent of blood in the water?

MAURICE. We're in an ugly mood this morning. Could it be because we slept with the poultry last night? I was invited. *(TOM regards GEMMA, suddenly reveals lost play and holds it over his head. Squints, awed.)* God, is it? Is it really it? *(TOM displays title page. MAURICE edges closer.)* Oh God, it is! *(Reads title.)* Autopsy of Love. There it is! That's it! It's real! This is worth millions. May I hold it?

TOM. No.

MAURICE. Touch it?

TOM. No.

MAURICE. Tom, please, you really don't get it, do you?

TOM. I really do, Maurice, get it.

MAURICE. *(Indicates manuscript.)* I can take that to London. Win; Easy Street, Gemma wears rubies, you get a new little pickup truck. Without it; no little pickup truck. You do want a little pickup truck that starts in the winter, don't you?

TOM. I like my little pickup truck as it is.

MAURICE. Great. You'll own a fleet of rusted little pickup trucks.

TOM. Sorry. I just don't care anymore.

MAURICE. Do it for Gemma.

TOM. *(States the obvious.)* She's leaving me.

MAURICE. But why?

TOM. *(Shows play.)* You're looking at it.

MAURICE. That? That's buried treasure.

TOM. Buried nuclear waste. Anyway, it won't hold up in court.

MAURICE. Why not? It's the original manuscript.

TOM. Anyone can go see Tomby and type it up. But these are definitely my coffee stains.

MAURICE. It's not copyrighted?

TOM. No.

GEMMA. *(To TOM, coolly.)* His life is his copyright.

MAURICE. *(In the dark.)* Is it? It is?

GEMMA. He can produce a witness.

MAURICE. He can?

TOM. *(Resignedly.)* It's the story of my life.

(Belatedly, the dawn rises on MAURICE.)

MAURICE. Oh, my God, Tom ... *Autopsy of Love* ... Tomby ....

TOM. Good morning, Maurice, I'm Tomby.

(A pause while MAURICE absorbs the obvious.)

MAURICE. Right.

(TOM tears the stained title page away and floats it toward the flames in the fireplace. It burns.)

TOM. Aged paper catches beautifully . .

MAURICE. Tomby, Tom, now don't joke, please, don't.

(MAURICE approaches TOM.)

TOM. Back, Maurice.

(TOM drops another page into the fire.)

MAURICE. Stop that. Stop him. It belongs to all of us. It belongs to history. Gemma, do something, it's your community property.

(Another page.)

TOM. This is where it belongs.

(Another page. And page-by-page, TOM drops the play script into the fireplace.)

MAURICE. You love to burn valuables, don't you? *(MAURICE lunges at it, grabs the air, falls in a heap. TOM drops the remaining pages onto the fire. It blazes. MAURICE crawls to the ashes, reaches in, picks up a few burning pages, singes his fingers, drops them back in fireplace, defeated.)* God, you're insane, on top of being crazy, I always knew it. *(MAURICE gets to his feet. He seems suddenly to have aged. He shuffles to the front door, buttoning his coat, barely nodding to GEMMA, who seems curiously oblivious of what they've just seen.)* I'll always hate you for this.
TOM. Hate's a big effort, Maurice.
MAURICE. You've got a good life, why set fire to your future?
TOM. You struck the match, Maurice.
MAURICE. *(Reverting.)* I'll see you in court, Tom, sue your ass.
TOM. Don't let another nineteen years go by before you destroy my life again. Why don't you give Emma a limousine ride to New York? *(TOM stands by the fireplace, GEMMA in the kitchen or somewhere in between. Knock at front door. MAURICE, his hand on the knob, turns it. ELI MORGENSTERN enters. All seem strangely relieved to see him.)* Hi, Eli.
ELI. Hi, Mr. Fairbrother. Hi, Mrs. Fairbrother. *(To MAURICE.)* Hi.

GEMMA. Hello, Eli.

(MAURICE ignores him. Everyone waits for ELI to speak. After a moment or two:)

TOM. What can I do for you, Eli?

ELI. Oh, nothin' much. Ted told me to bring this back to Mrs. Fairbrother. *(ELI upholds a 9 X 12 brown mailing envelope, size of the play script, addressed with stamps on it.)* He says you're a dollar short. *(Innocently.)* Ted says he can't mail it that way, so as long as I was heading back here, he says bring it to you and you could put on the extra dollar yourself. It's supposed to be two dollars and ninety cents and you got only one dollar and ninety cents on it, see?

GEMMA. *(Embarrassed.)* Oh, thank you, Eli.

ELI. He figured it's important or you wouldn't have been down there so early using his copy machine.

GEMMA. Thanks, Eli. For bringing it.

ELI. Oh, that's Okay, Mrs. Fairbrother.

(GEMMA holds her hand out for it.)

TOM. Who's it going to, Eli?

ELI. *(Stops, reads.)* Uhm Mister - Maurice - Bone - cream.

MAURICE. Me? Well how about that? I'll take delivery now, that's okay with you, isn't it, uh, Eli? I am Maurice Bonecream.

ELI. You got quite a name, sir.

(MAURICE has been digging for his business card.)

MAURICE. *(Warmly.)* Thank you. So do you, Eli. *(MAURICE holds his card against the envelope.)* See? That's me.

ELI. *(Puzzled.)* Yup, sure is. *(To GEMMA.)* Well, I guess you won't be needing those extra stamps. Want me to tear 'em off for you, Mrs. Fairbrother?

GEMMA. No!

(ELI hands MAURICE the envelope.)

MAURICE. What have we here, I wonder?

(MAURICE holds it up to the light, tears into it.)

TOM. *(At GEMMA.)* Take a wild guess.
MAURICE. What is it, Gemma? *(ELI hesitates by the front door to see if any of this will make sense. MAURICE holds the lost play.)* My God. *(He thumbs through it,* The Book of Kells. *Sighs in relief.)* It's the original copy! It's dirty, it's mildewed, it's ... copyrighted. Look, pencil scrawls.
TOM. *(To GEMMA.)* Why'd you mail it to him?
MAURICE. Because the Post Office doesn't burn mail?
TOM. Shut up, Maurice. *(To GEMMA.)* Why?
GEMMA. I phoned him late last night. He asked me, didn't I want a piece of the dream? I said, yes I did. So he told me to mail him the play for safekeeping, and make a copy for you.
TOM. I can't blame you, Gemma, you need decent clothes.
GEMMA. Well, I am a woman, after all, I may as well look it.
ELI. I think you look it, Mrs. Fairbrother.
GEMMA. Thanks, Eli.
MAURICE. So do I. Well, I'll be toddling along. *(MAURICE tries to exit. TOM takes a step toward him. ELI is accidentally blocking the door. MAURICE, sensing trouble, unfolds his tiny phone. Into phone)* Billy! Would you pop in here and give me a hand?
TOM. Must you go?
MAURICE. Yes, I'm running late.
TOM. Not you.
GEMMA. Yes, Tom.

(She finishes knotting string around a carton.)

TOM. It's okay, Maurice, you're safe. You're just an alien being from another galaxy.

MAURICE. I am your agent. I will always be your agent.

TOM. Go back to your planet.

MAURICE. I have a dream. Sue me.

TOM. Your dream is to have everything and still manage to be greedy.

MAURICE. *(Agreeably.)* You don't want to be rich. We do.

(TOM deftly grabs the envelope from MAURICE and presents it to GEMMA.)

TOM. With my compliments, Emma, I owe it to you.

(BILLY enters. MAURICE eyes play.)

MAURICE. *(Cautiously, to GEMMA.)* I'm only going as far as New York, may I offer you a lift?

GEMMA. I suppose you can.

MAURICE. Tell Billy which bags to load.

(GEMMA points to suitcase and carton, exits.)

TOM. You got your play.

MAURICE. We're even.

(MAURICE extends his hand, TOM lets it hang.)

TOM. Take it to London and give Emma the money. Now listen carefully, Maurice; if this play gets within fifty miles of Broadway, that includes Yonkers and Hoboken, this time you will die.

(MAURICE exits, followed by BILLY, carrying suitcase and carton. ELI and TOM are alone onstage.)

ELI. You know, Mr. Fairbrother, by the time you see the buzzard up there circling over your head, it's been watching you for a very long time.

Scene 2

(A couple of weeks later.
A fair day. TOM is alone onstage, except for ELI, who is slumped in a corner, engrossed in his freak gossip weekly. TOM is asleep over another copy. He wears socks with holes and a "Comfort Me with Cranberries" T-shirt. The mood is glum. Without GEMMA, the house is bleak. TOM seems very much alone.
Phone rings. ELI picks it up, starts to speak, listens instead.)

ELI. Okay, Mr. Bonecream. *(ELI hangs up, looks out window. TOM wakes.)* Mr. Bonecream is coming.

(TOM, still groggy, bellows to GEMMA upstairs.)

TOM. Emma? Throw down my thirty-dollar shoes?

(But of course there is no GEMMA. After a moment looking up, he wakes and gets into his boots.)

ELI. She's gone.
TOM. *(Wakes.)* I know that, Eli, I know that. Just kidding around. *(To himself.)* Why do I still do that?

(Rooster crows.)

ELI. Been gone weeks.
TOM. I know that! *(Suddenly, BONECREAM hurtles in, feverish.*

TOM is lacing up his boots as he bursts across the room.) Where in hell did you call from, the lawn?

MAURICE. Of course.

TOM. Whaddaya want?

MAURICE. That's not very simpatico is it, Tom?

TOM. What do you want?

MAURICE. Be that way.

TOM. How's my woman?

MAURICE. Gemma's fine. Still staying in my guest room.

TOM. Make sure she does.

MAURICE. Don't worry about her, Tom, she's still not quite ready to face life here. Last Saturday she went window shopping in the neighborhood and vanished for eight hours. I discovered her wandering outside Bergdorf Goodman's mumbling, Valentino, Valentino, a specie of lady's shoe. I got her over to a Bloomingdales sale on spring clothes and now she's working as my assistant at the office. She's recovering.

TOM. Recovering?

MAURICE. From you. She's becoming aware of a world without thrift shops, where women wear Italian shoes.

TOM. Thank you, Maurice. You have my wife. You have my play. Anything else? Look around, be sure, what about Eli?

MAURICE. I'm here to give, not to take.

TOM. You don't give, Maurice, remember?

MAURICE. I think you should let *Tomby* go to Broadway.

TOM. Never.

MAURICE. I'll tell you why ....

TOM. Don't bother.

MAURICE. It belongs there.

TOM. I wrote it to hurt someone. It still could.

MAURICE. *(Quickly.)* Call it *Autopsy of Love*.

TOM. They'd find out. *(Indicates* Enquirer.*)* Unknown Playwright Fakes Death. Why Is He Hiding?

MAURICE. Well, okay, let's just leave Sablehand's name on it.

TOM. That's another really good idea.

MAURICE. *(Misunderstanding.)* Good, let me cut the deal. We'll give him a percentage.

TOM. You cut a hard deal.

MAURICE. I think he'll sign.

TOM. Of course he'll sign, he's a plagiarist, remember? *(Suspiciously.)* You've been talking to him.

(MAURICE hems and haws, nods toward road.)

MAURICE. He's ... out there.

TOM. He's here? In Wadawanuck?

MAURICE. Shh! He's in the car. He doesn't know about our deal yet. He's not as smart as we are.

TOM. What deal? We don't have a deal. What's he doing in America?

MAURICE. He flew in to New York for the rehearsals.

TOM. Of — ?

MAURICE. Of you know.

TOM. Of *Tomby*.

MAURICE. Yes.

TOM. I'm going to kill you.

MAURICE. Of course, kill me, I wouldn't have it any other way, but first, hear me out. Then, if you must, you must.

TOM. You're willing to die for this?

(MAURICE unfolds his tiny phone, punches numbers, waits one second.)

MAURICE. Billy, would you ask Mr. Sablehand to step inside, please? *(To TOM.)* I thought he should meet you.

TOM. *(Flabbergasted.)* You did. What makes you think I won't kill him?

MAURICE. Kill-kill-kill, is that all you've got on your mind? I've been trying to convince him to pay us our royalties.

TOM. Convince him?

MAURICE. I'm afraid he doesn't believe you wrote it.

TOM. That's funny, I don't believe he wrote it.

(BILLY opens the door for DUNLOP SABLEHAND.

SABLEHAND looks every inch a British playwright: lean, engaging, fully maned, but curiously tanned. Royal. Flown in from England, apparently on ice, he is dressed for this countryside encounter wearing Himalayan mufti with epaulettes. He touches the doorframe for support.)

MAURICE. We're still a little tipsy, aren't we, Duny? *(SABLEHAND is conscious of his utterly writerly air. Constantly flicks strand of hair from brow. MAURICE, out of nervousness, is enjoying himself tremendously, vivacious from nerves; a delicate situation, an imminent deal.)* Tom, this is Dunlop Sablehand. Tom Vickery, my very first client, Dunlop Sablehand, my very last.

SABLEHAND. *(Engagingly.)* Extremely delighted to meet you, sir.

TOM. Sablehand, the pimp.

SABLEHAND. I ... the what?

MAURICE. *(Quietly.)* Tom, be nice.

TOM. Excuse me; the thief.

SABLEHAND. Here now, here, let's play fair.

MAURICE. We've been having fun, haven't we, Duny? *(To TOM.)* He read all the billboards in a funny voice. So many, I didn't realize, thousands, wish you'd been along, Tom.

SABLEHAND. Exactly. Absolutely refused to let me out of the car 'til I became a signed client of Bonecream Artists. I'm over the moon.

(They smile warmly at each other, client and parasite.)

MAURICE. Can you believe it? When he was a kid, he used to be my office boy. Now look.

TOM. An imposter.

MAURICE. Tom.

(SABLEHAND, who needs badly to urinate, hops foot-to-foot.)

SABLEHAND. Where would the loo be?

(TOM points to the kitchen door.)

TOM. The loo would be right out back there with a little half-moon over the door.

SABLEHAND. Quaint. *(Leaving, he turns.)* I have never wanted to visit Maine, and am here only as a kindness to my old mentor, Maurice Bonecream, at some inconvenience, to determine if there is one tittle of truth to support your claim, sir, of having contributed to my play, *Tomby*.

TOM. He's exactly as I imagined him! No, he's better. He's what the theater needs most. A British messenger, a facsimile of a dead culture we desperately envy, secretly fear, and will never grow ourselves.

SABLEHAND. I assure you, Mr. Fairbrother, or whatever your name happens to be this morning, I am no facsimile, I am an Englishman. Sablehands fell with Cromwell.

TOM. Not enough of them.

MAURICE. Please, Tom, Duny is different, okay? He's practically a royal, born in Knightsbridge with a silver spoon in his mouth.

TOM. And a silver fork up his twombini.

MAURICE. Tom?

SABLEHAND. I do not have to tolerate this sort of thing.

TOM. Yes, you do.

(SABLEHAND turns to MAURICE for a ruling. MAURICE shrugs, nods.)

MAURICE. *(Shrugs.)* You do.
SABLEHAND. As you wish.

(Can't stay a moment longer, exits to john.)

TOM. He's definitely not local.

(Rooster crows. TOM uncorks a bottle of cranberry cider, looks for glasses.)

MAURICE. You don't really use an out-house?
TOM. Na-ah, been there years. Tell you who does use it, a family of crow-eating spiders, they live just under the seat.
MAURICE. Crow-eating spiders?
TOM. Big as cats. They call 'em that because they ...
MAURICE. ... eat crows. *(Ref: trick.)* But why?
TOM. *(Ref: spiders.)* Hunger?
MAURICE. No, why did you do it?

(From the back yard, a lone sustained scream.)

TOM. *(Indicates SABLEHAND.)* Did you really sign that — item — on the way up here?

(TOM is pouring magenta fluid into three tumblers.)

MAURICE. I did, yes, I certainly did. I thought we could hammer out a mutually happy agreement and we did.

(They drink. SABLEHAND abruptly re-enters, zippering his trousers.

He shudders.)

SABLEHAND. Spiders, spiders. Huge spiders.

TOM. Damned spiders think they own the place. I bet one of 'em leapt at your ass.

SABLEHAND. *(Shaken.)* Exactly!

TOM. And missed.

SABLEHAND. Just.

TOM. Faulty vision.

SABLEHAND. They were bigger than ... cats. *(Realizing.)* If you were trying to assassinate me with your spiders, I am not amused. I came here to be shown evidence of your connection to *Tomby*. I have only been shown evidence of your mental disorder. I'll wait in the car.

(TOM is enjoying himself and SABLEHAND, who is washing in the sink.)

TOM. Isn't he wonderful?

MAURICE. Duny, sit down. Our play is this man's life story.

(MAURICE hands SABLEHAND a glass.)

SABLEHAND. Not that I dispute you, dear Maurice .. .

MAURICE. *(Slowly.)* Duny, Tom is Tomby in *Tomby*.

SABLEHAND. With all respect, the sign above the door says Thistledome.

MAURICE. That's the name of the house.

SABLEHAND. How sweet! Thistledome, delightful name for a cottage.

TOM. Not Thistledome. "This'll-Do-Me."

SABLEHAND. "This'll do me?" Thistledome? Oh, I get it. I see, I see. Super. Ha-ha. Excellent.

TOM. Put it in your next farce.

SABLEHAND. I shall. P'raps I shall. Marvelous. Thistledome, "This'll - Do - Me." Ha-ha.

TOM. By the way, what is a farce, Sablehand?

SABLEHAND. *(Trapped.)* Well, isn't it ... a fairly amusing situation?

TOM. Maybe in your case.

(ELI looks up from his reading.)

ELI. Mr. Fairbrother ?

(SABLEHAND leaps away, unaware of ELI.)

SABLEHAND. Who's that?

TOM. Eli. Yes, Eli?

ELI. *(Thickly.)* Isn't farce a well-constructed comedy wherein latitude is allowed as to the logic of its happenings within a skillfully exploited situation?

MAURICE. *(Unsure.)* I buy that, Eli. You, Tom?

TOM. I'm in. Sablehand?

SABLEHAND. *(Lost.)* Sounds right to me.

TOM. You twit, it's taken me about a minute to see you as the dim bulb you really are. It would take a lawyer less time to destroy you on the witness stand. You'd be laughed out of court, sued, fined, jailed and made to wear grownup clothes

SABLEHAND. I see.

TOM. So who wrote *Tomby*?

(After a moment, SABLEHAND capitulates, moans.)

SABLEHAND. I haven't the foggiest idea.

TOM. But it wasn't you.

SABLEHAND. No, not I.

(He seems to visualize humiliation lying just ahead.)

MAURICE. I think he sees the game's up, don't you Duny? But is court really the answer, Tom?

TOM. *(To MAURICE.)* Wouldn't turning him loose be a problem? *(To SABLEHAND.)* Being a celebrated first-time playwright, wouldn't your fans stand poised awaiting your second play? Your next landmark dark comedy? *Quo vadis*, Mr. Sablehand?

MAURICE. I was hoping we could talk sensibly.

TOM. How can we? Look at him. An empty taco.

MAURICE. He has ideas, Tom. Tell him your ideas, Duny.

TOM. Yes. Tell me your ideas.

SABLEHAND. *(Defensively.)* I don't have ideas?

TOM. You have other people's ideas.

(MAURICE prompts SABLEHAND.)

MAURICE. Tell him about your *Hamlet*.

SABLEHAND. Right. *Hamlet, the Musical*. The broken-hearted prince sings "Feelings."

(TOM watches SABLEHAND like a bug.)

MAURICE. *MacBeth*, tell him.

TOM. No.

MAURICE. *Porgy and Bess*. Go on, go on.

TOM. Yes, tell me your *Porgy and Bess*.

SABLEHAND. To offset its pervading Negro stigma ... an entirely white *Porgy and Bess*, set in Southport, Connecticut. Corky and Beth. Corky's just been laid off at the ad agency. Beth's from a distant harbor, Greenwich. Her real estate world has collapsed. These are burnt-out daily commuters. They meet at a yacht club dance. It's a magical, sweltering night, lit by fairy lights, the death of summer ....

TOM. Court!

SABLEHAND. Court?

TOM. Take him to court.

MAURICE. But court is in England.

TOM. Where he belongs and lawyers wear white toupees and evening gowns.

MAURICE. Stop, Tom, listen to me. *Tomby* belongs on Broadway.

TOM. *(To DUNY.)* So, why don't I get the ball rolling and write a letter to *The London Times* saying you didn't create *Tomby*?

SABLEHAND. *(Abruptly.)* Or why don't we do it another way? Why don't I simply confess all to *The New York Times*? That my inspiration for Tomby was you, Tom Vickery, and that I was merely trying to disguise your humiliating childhood. Shield you from your past.

MAURICE. Now, Duny.

SABLEHAND. Mayn't I do that? It should play well in Wappawanuck, or wherever we are. INCEST BOY BACK FROM DEAD? Death no fun without my Sis.

(People like yourself who read supermarket dreadfuls will be moved by my sacrifice. That I suppressed your curious love story to protect you.)

MAURICE. He could do it, Tom.

SABLEHAND. *(Directly to TOM.)* Let's get the truth out, I say. You're the one who seems to revere the truth so bloody much. Let them all hear your very pathetic biography.

TOM. Sorry that spider missed your ass.

(MAURICE dissolves into a chair, close to tears.)

MAURICE. This is a terrible situation. I don't honestly see a winner among us, I only see grief. Go after each other like this and we all lose, big. *(To TOM.)* You get a bad rap, Duny here gets exposed and ruined, I lose two clients.

TOM. You invertebrate. Sue him or I will.

(TOM approaches SABLEHAND. MAURICE sandwiches his body between them.)

SABLEHAND. Gentlemen, there's nothing left to sue me for. It's all gone. I was swindled. The Uberlanders owned everything — theater, box office, production. They invented phantom costs, profits vanished. Their bookkeeping would make Rembrandt weep. I don't have a penny.

MAURICE. It's the truth, Tom, I checked. We've all been done. Duny doesn't owe you a cent. You're broke, he's broke. Can't we just relax and make some money?

TOM. And once he makes his reputation on Broadway there'll be no limit to the amount of rubbish you two can peddle.

MAURICE. He's not a playwright, remember? This is a one-shot deal, I swear. *(To SABLEHAND.)* You'll never do this again, right Duny?

SABLEHAND. As long as I live.

TOM. At least with greed you always know where you stand, right Maurice?

MAURICE. Right!

SABLEHAND. Shall we proceed?

MAURICE. Oh, please. *(TOM hesitates.)* Tom, at Bergdorf Goodman's a single pair of Valentino's sling-back high-heel pumps cannot be had for less than four-hundred-and-twenty-nine dollars.

TOM. If I only knew.

(About his sister, SHELLEY. MAURICE holds his arm, looks into his

eyes.)

MAURICE. Tom, you'll know.

(This is a mysterious moment, a prelude to MAURICE's spiritual ascension in the final scene.)

TOM. *(Nods assent.)* Keep my name off it.
MAURICE. Yes!

(He executes a tight, involuntary jeté. Recovers, unfolds a crisp letter of agreement. Produces pen.)

MAURICE. We'll keep your name off it.

(TOM scans the page.)

TOM. *(Indicates SABLEHAND.)* This one gets ten-percent?
MAURICE. We give Duny nine-percent of the author's share. After all, without him ....
TOM. Let's go to Broadway.

(TOM scrawls his name on letter. MAURICE crumples happily.)

Scene 3

Dawn. Several weeks later. First yellow sunlight through the windows. House in early stage of decay
Evidence of a new product. A rude, newly painted sign proclaims:

```
Grandpa sez —
"Fairbrother BRANDY
Tastes Better'n CANDY."
```

(TOM, wearing bedspread and the earlier socks, is on phone listening. He seems to be alone in house. No ELI. A clear-glass bottle of Fairbrother Brandy stands empty on the table. Beside it, another one holding the final ounces of the magenta fluid. TOM wields an empty glass. Each time he hears a sentence on the telephone, he will repeat it.)

TOM. I can sense here a truly powerful love story, star-crossed, deep in its desolation ... *(Listens.)* ... yet joy came over me. As if against all odds in this cockeyed world, these two kids found a sliver of hope and for a few moments lived within a deeper love.... Was that *The Times? (Listen.)* Someone's wife wrote it. *(Listens.)* The director's wife. She posted it backstage on the call board. What else you got there? *(Listens.)* This is a case where the laughter drowned out a great love story. *(Listens.)* Okay. Was that *The Times*? *(Listens.) The Nyack Intelligencer. (Listens.)* ... riveted to my seat? Sounds painful. Where's *The Times*? *(Listens.)* Find. The. Times. *(Listens.)* Not angry at you. No! Please Don't hang up, Mr. Pinnochio.... *(Listens.)* Riccaccio, excuse me, Mr. Riccaccio, I know you're busy, but could you try to look for *The New York Times*, please? *(Listens.)* Flowers scattered everywhere backstage. Sounds like a real mess. They're not neat people, actors. *(Listens.)* Okay, pigs. Just sweep the flowers in a pile. Teach 'em grace. *(Listens.) Humility. (Listens.)* Sablehand's unsteady vision claims ... best lovers are made by blood relatives ... becomes progressively clearer that today's morals .... *(Listens.)* Next. *(Listens.)* Try dressing rooms, ladies room, men's room. Go on in.... *(Listens.)* Don't walk on the broken bottles! *(Listens.)* If she's not in her dressing room, look in her bathroom.

(Listens.) I see no logical reason to review this carnival of smut. I can't go on.... *(Laughs.)* That wasn't *The Times*, was it? *(Listens.)* On the wall ... in lipstick. *(Listens, relieved.)* It's not a suicide note, if there's no body, Mr. Riccacccio. *(Suddenly excited.)* The *Times*? *(Listens, droops.)* In the toilet? Is it too wet to read? *(Listens.)* Yes, please ... do you mind just ...? *(Listens.)* I know you're not a plumber, Mr. Riccaccio, and I wouldn't ask you, except that human life depends on it.... *(Listens.)* Stick it to the wall, you know, flatten it out, it'll dry. *(Waits, laughs nervously.)* I know just what you mean, Mr. Boccaccio, I wear glasses, too, what a coincidence. *(Waits.)* Last night — a vile odor emanated — from the alley behind the Booth Theatre — spreading toxic fumes along 44th Street between 6th and 7th Avenues.... *(Listens.)* These fumes are called — *Tomby*.... *(To himself.)* This is not sounding like a money review. *(Listens, wilts.)* There is no known grouping for *Tomby* and I would like my readers — to remember that title — for it has set new limits in theatre for — filth. *Stop*! Thank you. *(Listens, wearily.)* No, I'm not upset at you, Mr. Riccaccio. Go home, take the flowers to your wife, celebrate, have a nap, then later on; maybe a little job hunting. *(TOM hangs up PHONE, crumples.)*

Jesus, it's all over. *(TOM, utterly beaten, slumps against wall. He never wanted this success for himself, only for GEMMA, but now he's lost it all; something he never had. He drinks from his too-empty glass. Raving.)* He destroyed my play. He loved destroying it. Toxic fumes? He destroyed it with imagery. *(Grandly.)* Deliver me from critics! No known grouping for this play? Give them groupings, no surprises. Tell them what it is so they know how to feel. They can never speak first, they must wait, voyeurs at Venetian blinds, they know all about sex but have never actually penetrated anyone. *(He careens toward the kitchen area and empties the bottle into his glass. Toasts Grandpa sez sign.)* There is no known grouping for this fluid. Cranberry brandy's never been attempted before. They can't touch that! *(Drinks. Reels. Raving in grand performance.)* The critics enter

Wadawanuck; *(Indicates brandy.)* This vicious fluid has a severely disappointing nose. Its color, alizarin red, betrays an odious pulse, curiously devoid of integrity…. *(Looks toward ceiling.)* Even the birds in Wadawanuck sing with no restraint and little sense of ….

(BUM! BUM! BUM! BUM! BUM! BUM! BUM! BUM! BUM! BUM! Noise! Throbbing, thrumming from above. It grows louder and louder. Plates rattle. A picture falls. TOM throws himself to floor, crawls to window, peers out. Helicopter is apparently idling twenty feet above on the road out front. The rooster crows.
Phone rings, barely heard above noise. TOM slithers to phone. It is MAURICE requesting permission to land. TOM shouts above din.)

TOM. *(Listens.)* Maurice? *(Listens.)* Request a WHAT? *(Listens.)* Permission to land? Land, for God's sake. LAND! Permission granted.

(TOM slithers back to window and watches the landing. Rotors are cut. Rooster crows.
Soon an exuberant MAURICE is standing in doorway, throbbing from his experience, helmet in hand, or admiral's cap on head. Gold accessories are absent.)

MAURICE. Whom were you expecting? Miss Saigon?

(MAURICE enjoys his joke. TOM does not, remains in a defensive crouch.)

TOM. You could have called.
MAURICE. I did. That was me.
TOM. No, earlier. Before. *(Indicates henhouse.)* Hens are shaken, won't lay eggs for a month.

MAURICE. You want eggs? I'll send you a case.

TOM. Not CITY, my eggs.

MAURICE. Apologize to them for me, I have a higher purpose. I needed to come.

TOM. By helicopter?

MAURICE. Client gave it to me in lieu of a commission. It's a converted Iraqi [or Arab] gunship, captured in Desert Storm. Ever flown 250 miles in a war prize?

TOM. No.

MAURICE. *(Macho.)* You'll know it when you do.

TOM. *(Touched by effort.)* Look, Maurice, thanks for coming but don't worry about me. I saw *The Times.*

MAURICE. Exactly why I'm here.

TOM. *(Shrugs, sadly.)* Emma just lost something she never had. She'll be Okay.

MAURICE. *(Trying to contain excitement.)* I'll say she'll be okay. Your advance sale between midnight and 6 a.m. is a hundred-sixty-one-thousand dollars and rising. A Broadway record for a straight play. *(He pauses exquisitely.) Nobody liked it but the people.*

TOM. Huh?

MAURICE. *(Grandly.)* The people spokes.

TOM. *(Lost.)* What did they say?

MAURICE. They said *YES. (MAURICE unballs a grubby print-out.)* Print-out of advance sales at the box office. We've got a hit, partner.

TOM. How?

MAURICE. It all began on the Eleven O'clock News. That blonde bimbo — Helen Running-Wolf. *(Quotes from memory.) Tomby ripped the top of my head away — literally blew the lid off my psyche.*

TOM. *(Uncertain.)* That's favorable?

MAURICE. Of course it's favorable. She said you ground her into an emotional paste.

TOM. How can that be good?

MAURICE. That's as good as it gets. They want that to happen to them.

TOM. But she'll be okay.

MAURICE. *(Patiently.)* Yeah, she'll be fine. She got it started but it was the shooting that put us over the top.

TOM. The shooting?

MAURICE. You don't have television up here? You live like a shut-in. *(Savoring the tale.)* John Grosz, the *Daily News* critic, went berserk at Elaine's. He ran out screaming, *Arrest me! Arrest me! Tomby is my life story! I have sinned against nature!* You touched a nerve, pal. Luckily an occupied police car was parked out front and he threw many cobblestones through its windows. The cops simply returned fire. At Roosevelt Hospital they extracted eight slugs from his midsection out of politeness, and just left the rest for later. *(Trembling with excitement.)* He's not going to pull through, Tom.

TOM. Oh, my God. That's *not* good. Right?

MAURICE. *(Controlling himself, slowly.)* A first-string critic is no longer living as a result of seeing your play. *IT DOESN'T GET ANY BETTER THAN THAT.*

TOM. I just see one more victim of incest.

MAURICE. And a very restless one he was, too.

(GEMMA and SABLEHAND sort of stagger in quietly behind TOM, arm-in-arm, wobbly from the flight. TOM isn't aware of them. SABLEHAND has been air-sick, but looks affluent in a suit similar to MAURICE's. GEMMA is a lovely vision in a summer suit with a short, pleated skirt, light pumps. Her hair is different. She seems to be about twelve.)

TOM. Have they connected me to his death?

MAURICE. *(Gravely.)* The Grosz family has requested the playwright's appearance at the memorial service.

(TOM crumples with an oath in a chair.)

    SABLEHAND. That'll be me.

(TOM turns and gapes.)

    TOM. *(Brightens.)* It will?
    MAURICE. It'll land us on the cover of *People Magazine*.
    GEMMA. *(Quietly.)* Hello, Tom.
    TOM. Emma! *(To SABLEHAND.)* Get your hands off my wife, Sablehand.
    GEMMA. I'm holding him up.
    SABLEHAND. Rough crossing. Hear about Grosz? Good show.
    TOM. You twit. *(To GEMMA.)* What are you doing here?
    GEMMA. Maurice asked me if I'd ever seen New England from the air.
    TOM. Now you have. *(Seriously.)* What brought you back, Emma, the play?
    GEMMA. I won't tell you. *(Indicates MAURICE.)* He has a surprise for you.

(TOM turns with a deadly look at MAURICE.)

    TOM. You have a surprise, Maurice?
    MAURICE. I do indeed. *(Rhetorically.)* Now where is Eli?
    TOM. Where should he be? He drove to Portland last night for *The Times*.
    MAURICE. *(He knows better.)* Oh, he did, did he? And he's not back yet?

(TOM looks out window, checks road for the pickup.)
    TOM. *(Worried.)* Pickup's still gone. Funny.

MAURICE. Is it a small tired truck with pictures of berries painted on its sides?

SABLEHAND. And brown trim on the bonnet?

TOM. Rust.

SABLEHAND. We spotted it from the air.

MAURICE. Limping toward the house, a mile down the road. *(There's the sound of blown exhaust through a perforated muffler, dangling parts, a weary motor coming to rest. MAURICE looks out window.)* It made it.

TOM. *(To GEMMA.)* You said you welded the muffler.

GEMMA. I said I was going to.

MAURICE. *(Good naturedly.)* Get yourself a new truck, Tom, get three, get a dozen weary little rusted trucks with berries painted ....

(Knock on the door. Before anyone can speak, the door swings open and ELI has wheeled in SHELLEY. She is in a wheelchair. She is a slim, handsome woman with her gray hair pulled straight back. She reminds one of a middle-aged Kate Hepburn. The reason for the wheelchair is never explained. In a wordless, graceful motion, ELI scoops her up out of her wheelchair and places her comfortably on the sofa. An easy rapport has already been established between the two.
SHELLEY and TOM study each other. He takes a step.)

TOM. Who's that?

SHELLEY. *(Quietly.)* Tomby.

(TOM takes his time, figuring.)

TOM. Shelley. My God, you're ... alive.

(TOM is in shock, SHELLEY has been able to prepare.)

SHELLEY. So are you. I'm sorry about ... well, my abrupt

departure.

    TOM. Oh, that, well, that couldn't be helped.

    SHELLEY. I know.

    TOM. Maybe a postcard would have been nice.

    SHELLEY. I hope I didn't upset you.

    TOM. No. Time to cut the cord. What happened to you?

    SHELLEY. Nothing much. I'll tell you one day.

    TOM. No big hurry.

    SHELLEY. I loved your play. It made me cry.

(TOM looks at MAURICE whose eyes are brimming.)

    TOM. You read it?

    SHELLEY. Yes. I'm glad you're alive. Hello, Tom.

    TOM. Hello, Shelley, welcome back.

(He breaks the emotion, laughs loudly.)

    SHELLEY. Come here, baby, don't be shy, sit down.

(TOM glances at GEMMA, who seems tense, then goes to SHELLEY. Hugs her, kisses her, kneels. MAURICE seems to be undergoing some subtle changes.)

    TOM. I'm very much alive.

    SHELLEY. So Maurice tells me. *(To MAURICE.)* God bless you, Mr. Bonecream.

    TOM. God *bless* Maurice?

    GEMMA. He found Shelley.

    TOM. Did he, Eli?

    ELI. *(Nods.)* Yup.

    TOM. How?

    GEMMA. *(To TOM.)* He took out ads in newspapers that said

Shelley was heiress to a fortune. Notified banks, ran credit tracers.

TOM. Where?

GEMMA. She turned up fifty miles from this very spot. She's living in East India at Sighing Oaks. It's a residential ....

(TOM realizes it's a euphemism for "rest home.")

TOM. *(Interrupts.)* What are you doing in a place like that?

SHELLEY. Good people. They look after you at Sighing Oaks. Minimum security.

TOM. Why are those places always named after trees?

SHELLEY. *Sighing* trees.

GEMMA. Maurice did a lovely thing and never said a word.

MAURICE. *(To TOM.)* You're having trouble dealing with that.

TOM. I am. Trouble believing it.

GEMMA. And Maurice did it all in secret. I'll never get over it.

ELI. I guess your real friends do favors behind your back, huh.

TOM. What's come over you, Maurice?

MAURICE. I ....

SHELLEY. He said he wouldn't do the play of I didn't want him to.

GEMMA. *(To SHELLEY.)* Can I tell him what you told me? No, you tell him.

(SHELLEY touches TOM or, if he's kneeling, cradles his head. She takes a breath.)

SHELLEY. I visited Mom after your death. A long time ago. We both felt so sick about it. Total despair. I told her about ... us.

(Unnoticed, MAURICE signals SABLEHAND, they slip out kitchen door. But ELI makes no move to leave, watches SHELLEY protectively. He has been standing apart, looking after her

throughout the scene, fascinated by someone so wonderful being confined to such a small world.)

TOM. You did?

(SHELLEY nods. With GEMMA, TOM and SHELLEY form a triangle.)

SHELLEY. It just came out. It didn't matter anymore. For some odd reason I wanted her to know about us.
TOM. What did she say?
SHELLEY. Well, nothing at first, she was shocked, of course. Then she told me something she'd always kept secret. I was adopted.
TOM. You? Adopted? I can't believe it. She never told me.

(TOM laughs freely for the first time.)

SHELLEY. I'm really the daughter of her dear friend and neighbor, Anne O'Meara, who died after a car wreck. Mom swore to her in the hospital she'd raise me as her own.
TOM. This happened before Mom married Dad?
SHELLEY. Yeah. I always wondered about those dates.

(GEMMA hesitates, puts an arm around TOM.)

TOM. You knew?
GEMMA. *(Moved, nods.)* Since yesterday.
SHELLEY. When Mom told me, I felt free.
TOM. So do I. It's *not* blood, Shelley. God, what's thicker than blood?
ELI. Oatmeal?
SHELLEY. But what difference does it make after all these years? *(Feels tension.)* Does it?

TOM. Does it Emma?

GEMMA. We need to talk, Tom, about everything.

TOM. There's almost nothing I know for sure, but I do know I'll always love you, Shelley, my sister, and I'll always be *in* love with you Emma, my wife.

(He still holds SHELLEY's hand while he stands to embrace GEMMA. SHELLEY sees that TOM and GEMMA need to be alone, turns to ELI who has been studying her.)

SHELLEY. Eli, would you like to show me around the property, please?

ELI. Want to see where I live?

SHELLEY. I would be delighted.

(ELI picks up SHELLEY, sets her back in wheelchair.)

ELI. Well, half a mystery is better than a full mystery.

SHELLEY. *(Reflects.)* That's true. You're a little off center, Eli, I can tell.

ELI. I guess.

SHELLEY. Well, so am I.

(He wheels her toward back door, turns to group.)

ELI. We'll be back soon.

(GEMMA waits for door to close. They are alone. She crosses to TOM, hugs him.)

GEMMA. Isn't she wonderful? She's so ... different than I pictured her.

TOM. More disabled?

GEMMA. No!

TOM. And I'm not in love with her. I know that.

GEMMA. And it's not incest, Tom.

TOM. No, it's not incest.

GEMMA. And as far as I'm concerned she's just one of your old girlfriends.

(TOM says nothing.)

GEMMA. It's all different now, but you have years of explaining to do, years of deceit to account for, Tom.

TOM. Do you think you can ever trust me?

GEMMA. It'll take me years to feel sure of you again. Is there anything left to lie to me about?

TOM. No, that's the last of it.

GEMMA. Isn't it *the* most wonderful news you could imagine?

(TOM and GEMMA are almost kissing when MAURICE and SABLEHAND re-enter from front door. It's clear a powerful event has just gone down.)

MAURICE. *Beaut-tiful* sunrise.

SABLEHAND. Exactly.

MAURICE. Where are —?

TOM. Touring the grounds.

GEMMA. *(About ELI.)* He's taken quite a shine to her.

TOM. Can't blame him. She's turned into a great lady.

MAURICE. Ah. *(There's a rich embarrassing silence.)* Well, shall we get the wine in here. Duny? *(DUNY snaps open a tiny phone.)* I feel a toast coming on.

SABLEHAND. *(Into phone.)* Mr. Bravo, would you bring in the wine?

MAURICE. *(Making small talk.)* So, how do you find your

sister?

TOM. I'm glad to meet her again.

GEMMA. Thanks to Maurice.

TOM. *(Starting to believe.)* Thanks to Maurice.

MAURICE. I was delighted she liked your play.

TOM. In your ads, you mentioned her being an heiress?

MAURICE. Oh, yes. But only a device to find her, Tom, a gag. I'm good at finding people.

(Knock at front door. SABLEHAND admits a unique personage. YO BRAVO. A beribboned gunner remaindered from Desert Storm. YO is in motley; an interpretation of desert fatigues combined with soldier of fortune. YO carries a case of champagne and half a dozen glass flutes. YO is macho.)

BRAVO. Yo! I'm Yo Bravo, Desert Storm. Don't mind I crash your debriefing.

(Distracted hellos and heys, here and there.)

MAURICE. Thanks, Yo, pop a cork for us, please, and pour the wine.

BRAVO. *Sir.*

(YO takes case to kitchen, pries it open with issue survival knife. SHELLEY and ELI re-enter. He easily picks her up and makes her comfortable on the sofa. He is deeply touched by SHELLEY.)

TOM. See his cottage?

SHELLEY. Such a pretty ... habitat. Eli lives like a raccoon.

ELI. Thanks, Shelley.

TOM. He built it mainly for our weekly poker game.

SHELLEY. You play poker, Eli?

ELI. I do, Shelley. You?

SHELLEY. *(Nods.)* I suspect you play a weak hand very well.

ELI. I try.

SHELLEY. Let's both try. That's all we can do.

ELI. Well, when the lights go out, the blind keep moving.

(SHELLEY absorbs the compliment.)

SHELLEY. *(Vaguely.)* Yes. Thank you, Eli.

(YO pops a second cork, sending a spire of foam toward the kitchen ceiling. SABLEHAND, a born butler, pours and serves. The six raise their glasses. Wait for someone to toast.)

TOM. Eli?

ELI. *Need* what you already have.

(They touch glasses and drink.)

TOM. *(Affectionately.)* What are you going to do with the rest of your life, Maurice?

MAURICE. Me? Oh, I roll on. Old Man River.

TOM. But what do you want?

MAURICE. I'll be fine as is, Tom, no entrepreneur ever went broke being sincerely mediocre.

TOM. Isn't there anything you really want beside money?

MAURICE. *(Suddenly animated.)* Can I be honest with you?

TOM. Give it a shot, Maurice, let's see if you can.

MAURICE. I've always wanted to be a producer. The *word* alone excites me physically: Pro-Du-Cer.

TOM. What's stopping you?

MAURICE. People don't trust me.

TOM. That's never been a criterion, look at the Uberlanders.

MAURICE. I've made enemies.

TOM. I wonder why.

ELI. Mr. Fairbrother?

TOM. What is it, Eli?

ELI. Well, why can't the three of you work together? *(To TOM.)* Why don't you write another play, Mr. Fairbrother? Mr. Sablehand could sign his name to it. And why doesn't Mr. Bonecream produce it? That way *(TOM)* you'd get paid to write it in nameless secrecy and *(SABLEHAND)* you'd keep your reputation, plus a commission, and *(MAURICE)* you'd become a producer and get a commission too, and *(GEMMA)* Mrs. Fairbrother could get her shoes from Boston.

TOM. Rome.

(To TOM's knowledge, this is the longest sentence ELI has uttered since his fall. The three men regard one another with various degrees of awe. It is a brilliant solution, considering the source.)

MAURICE. *(To ELI.)* What's in it for you, kid?

ELI. *(Sheepishly, even for ELI.)* I've always wanted to direct.

MAURICE. To *direct*? Direct what?

ELI. Plays?

MAURICE. What are your credentials?

ELI. One year, Yale Drama School.

MAURICE. Do you still harbor contempt for the audience?

ELI. I can learn to accept their presence in the theater.

MAURICE. Then you shall direct!

SABLEHAND. What's our first opus to be?

MAURICE. What about your white *Porgy and Bess?*

TOM. *(Controlled.)* No, Maurice.

MAURICE. What about your black *Showboat?*

TOM. *(Suppressing scream.) NO*! I mean; no.

MAURICE. I could get Pavarotti for the part of the slave ... you know, Jim? He could sing *Ol' Man River.*

SABLEHAND. But Pavarotti is ....

TOM. White?

SABLEHAND. Exactly.

TOM. Yes, he is, you bimbo. And Captain Andy's going to be black.

MAURICE. It's never good unless it's a little scary, Tom.

TOM. Not this scary.

MAURICE. Well, do *you* have any ideas?

TOM. What about ... a farce? *(Scrambling.)* New York City. Office boy finds play hidden under old files. Steals it. It's a dark comedy about incest, unknown, never produced. Kid hangs on to it, doesn't know why. Years pass. London. Now the kid's an agent, rediscovers play, reads it. It knocks him cold, very contemporary. Whose play is it? No one's. Author's long dead. Kid thinks *Why not say I wrote it?* He puts his name on it, changes title, shows it to a producer. After all, the play never even existed. Now it's his!

SABLEHAND. *(Doesn't get it.)* Sounds ripping. I'd sign my name to that.

TOM. I know.

MAURICE. I'd produce it.

ELI. I'd direct it.

TOM. I'd write it.

SABLEHAND. But why does it all sound so familiar?

MAURICE. Because ....

TOM. Don't.

MAURICE. *(Nods, turns to ELI and SHELLEY.)* Now what I can do for you?

(ELI takes SHELLEY's hand.)

ELI. You've done enough for now, Mr. Bonecream.

MAURICE. Whatever, you're nice kids. *(He looks around him to include TOM and GEMMA.)* You're all nice kids, wonderful,

wonderful people.

(Not in the style of the play: A special light comes up on MAURICE. He is in a private golden aura. He resembles an angel. He speaks as if attached to a higher plane.)

MAURICE. *(To SHELLEY and ELI.)* Why don't I give you my *entire* commission from *Tomby?*

(No one understands. Stunned, SHELLEY turns to ELI for interpretation.)

ELI. Play, movie, video, coffee mugs, T-shirts, I want you to have it all.

(TOM is stunned. Does some emphatic action.)

TOM. *(Warily.)* Why?

(MAURICE realizes what he's said, falters, recovers.)

MAURICE. *(Absolutely lost.)* I don't know, but I *mean* it.
TOM. I don't get it.
MAURICE. I don't get it either, believe me, Tom, I feel like I'm in the grip of something ... under orders from ... stronger forces.

(TOM has become seriously concerned about MAURICE.)

TOM. Does it feel ... okay?
MAURICE. Does it feel okay. I'll tell you how it feels: It's new to me. It's giving away commissions, you follow?
TOM. *(Trying.)* I think I follow. You're now in a larger metaphor.
MAURICE. There's no precedent.

ELI. Is it like God, or something?

MAURICE. *(Reflecting.)* Yeah, Eli. A little like God, a little like krypton. I feel like ... giving ... all of a sudden.

ELI. It feels good, doesn't it?

MAURICE. It's giving, how good can that feel? It feels like beetles are gnawing my private parts from the inside.

ELI. Is it that painful?

MAURICE. Yes, but it's not a sharp pain yet, it's not an ache, just a gnawing. What are you, a nurse? *(To TOM.)* What have you got up here? Jolly beans in the drinking water?

SHELLEY. Maybe it's penance.

MAURICE. Penance? For what? I'm an agent. I dedicate my life to helping people. *(He cracks.)* No, no, that's not true, I'm a *worthless check, a hopeless wreck, a flop* ....

ELI. Cole Porter.

MAURICE. Right! And all I've ever done is take. Take, take, take.

SHELLEY. Haven't you ever given? Not even once?

MAURICE. Never, not once. I've always been a people-people-person, you know, someone who hates to be alone. That's why I became an agent, so people would talk to me, ask my advice. All my life I put myself close to people I admire but when they got off the elevator, I was left alone at the end of the ride, at the end of the day, alone, not wanting to be alone.

(He is on the verge of tears.)

SHELLEY. We don't hate you. *(Looks around.)* Do we?

OTHERS. *(A murmured chorus:)* No.

MAURICE. You grow berries. You sew tapestries. You do whatever it is you do.

ELI. Roofing.

MAURICE. Whatever. I don't earn my money, understand?

Maybe I look like I do but I don't. I introduce people at lunch. I'm an agent. *(Cracks.)* And I like it.

TOM. Don't feel bad, Maurice, I'm an agent, too.

MAURICE. *(Refusing comfort.)* You're a what? You're not a agent Tom, I'm an agent. You're a grower, you create.

TOM. You're wrong. Do you really think I *create* cranberries? I couldn't create a cranberry in a thousand lifetimes. I guide them but they take care of growing themselves. I'm an agent. I have one client. I represent a common miracle called growth.

MAURICE. *(Sobbing.)* That's beautiful. I think. *(To TOM.)* Would you mind holding me?

TOM. I would very much mind holding you.

MAURICE. I understand. *(Looks around.)* Someone?

(GEMMA is about to offer. SABLEHAND sees his opening.)

SABLEHAND. I'll hold him.

(SABLEHAND hugs him. Son-father. MAURICE sobs.)

MAURICE. I'm a sycophant, a puppet, a toy person.

TOM. *(To ALL.)* Remember this. The rarest sight you'll ever see; a sobbing agent.

GEMMA. You did a lovely thing, Maurice, you changed our lives.

TOM. You sure did.

MAURICE. *(Still on.)* A cartoon, a balloon.

SHELLEY. Oh, shut up, you're practically a saint.

(MAURICE gently breaks free from the SABLEHAND hug.)

MAURICE. *(Emerging.)* Saint? Saint Maurice?

SABLEHAND. *(Like MAURICE.)* St. Moritz.

MAURICE. Much better. *(To ELI and SHELLEY.)* I meant what I said. I intend to turn over all my profits from *Tomby* to you kids. You're my witnesses.

SABLEHAND. Bravo!

MAURICE. We go back, Duny, how many years?

SABLEHAND. Twenty, not counting the nineteen-year separation. I looked up to you then.

MAURICE. *Why*?

SABLEHAND. I aspired to be like you one day.

MAURICE. *(Dejected.)* And look at you. See how you turned out? Like me.

SABLEHAND. *(Misunderstanding.)* Thanks, Mr. Bonecream.

(Something right suddenly clicks in between them. One couldn't see it before.)

MAURICE. I was fond of you then, my ambitious little office boy — devious, unprincipled, spoiled. You could hardly read in those days and you still can't. You need schooling, Duny. I wonder if I could legally adopt you ... and pass the Bonecream *baton* on to you.

SABLEHAND. It's a fine legacy, sir, I'd like that.

(SABLEHAND is a toady but he is a gentleman toady.)

MAURICE. I thought you might. *(MAURICE mists briefly as he gazes toward a new day.)* Bonecream and Sablehand.

SABLEHAND. *Bonecream and Sablehand,* Lord, yes, they do fit curiously well together.

MAURICE. And God knows I've never had anyone to look after, beside myself. That's been my downfall.

ELI. I've never had anyone either.

MAURICE. *(Reflectively.)* Not many people have.

(YO BRAVO has found himself a glass and has been weeping listlessly

in a corner of the kitchen.)

BRAVO. Yo! *Me neither.* Negative!

SABLEHAND. I never even knew my own papa [pa-pah]. I always wondered who …..

(MAURICE has a sudden revelation. He faces SABLEHAND squarely with double eye contact, speaks slowly.)

MAURICE. Did your mother visit Paris one chilly October thirty-six years ago?

(Everyone in the room realizes, even ELI. They wait impatiently for DUNY to think. Could it be possible …?)

SABLEHAND. No.
MAURICE. *Think.*
SABLEHAND. No.

(MAURICE is crestfallen but strangely relieved.)

MAURICE. Na-ah, I suppose not.

(MAURICE's special fades.)

SABLEHAND. *(Hasn't been following.)* Mummy kept a cottage in Blackpool. Why d'you ask?
MAURICE. Forget it. *(To BRAVO.)* Kick it over, Mister Bravo, let's go home.
BRAVO. *Sir!*

(BRAVO bucks up, exits.)

TOM. Maurice, well, thanks, I guess I needed that. Stay in touch.

MAURICE. I'll say I will. Know what a fax machine is?

TOM. *(Blankly.)* Fax machine?

MAURICE. *(As a producer.)* You'll see one over there ... *(kitchen table)* tomorrow. Read the booklet. I'll need some pages Wednesday, Tom.

TOM. I'm not Tom. I'm Halen.

MAURICE. *(Realizes.)* So you won't be coming to New York.

TOM. *(Shakes head.)* Nope.

(Roar close to house as rotor kicks in.)

MAURICE. *(Engagingly.)* Gemma? Flying back with us?

(TOM and GEMMA have been fondling each other like chimps. She detaches herself.)

GEMMA. I'm afraid I'm still married, dear Maurice, and I need to discuss mental infidelity with my husband. After I've done that, we may discuss breeding. Next year I'll be running for mayor of Wadawanuck, try to keep those schlock food franchises off our street. But maybe I can drag him down to your Big Apple once in awhile to see how bad it can get. Will your guest room be available?

MAURICE. *(Beaming.)* Of course.

(TOM leads GEMMA toward the stairs.)

TOM. Will you excuse us?

MAURICE. You don't need to explain.

(They are climbing the stairs.)

TOM. God, I hope not.

(GEMMA is at the bedroom door, turns.)

GEMMA. Goodbye, Maurice, you're a *godsend.*

(She closes bedroom door behind them.
The special briefly comes up again on MAURICE. Perhaps a solemn
flourish of organ music.)

MAURICE. *(To no one.)* Godsend? I wonder. *(MAURICE smiles,*
then shakes his head, "na-a-ah," and the special quickly flickers out.
To SABLEHAND.) Let's get outta here before I buy land.
SABLEHAND. Right you are, Mr. Bonecream.

(MAURICE bends and hugs SHELLEY. SABLEHAND shakes both
ELI's hands warmly.)

MAURICE. *(To bedroom door.)* Goodbye up there!

(Muffled goodbyes from above. MAURICE and SABLEHAND Exit.
Rooster crows.
ELI and SHELLEY are alone onstage. ELI refills their glasses.)

ELI. They crack the mold *before* they make the really good ones.
SHELLEY. Yes, they do.

(In a few moments roar of helicopter has faded and silence has
descended once again upon Thistledome.)

ELI. You play the violin?
SHELLEY. I do, Eli, an excellent guess.
ELI. I was hoping you did.

(ELI touches SHELLEY.)
SHELLEY. Eli, what are *you* going to do with the rest of your

life?

ELI. Look after you?

SHELLEY. I'd like that.

ELI. I would, too, Shelley, I never had anyone I wanted to look after.

SHELLEY. Not many people do.

(They are startled by each other's being and the abrupt rightness of their propinquity.)

ELI. What about moving into my cottage with me?

SHELLEY. I'd love it.

ELI. We could live like raccoons.

SHELLEY. We'll need curtains. *(ELI refills their glasses.)* Well, now, why don't we drive back over to Sighing Oaks and pick up my things?

ELI. And your violin.

SHELLEY. And my violin.

(ELI glows. He wheels her toward the door.)

ELI. Did you really speak to your mom before she died?

SHELLEY. I did, yes, Eli.

ELI. About your being adopted?

SHELLEY. We didn't get around to that.

ELI. Do you think you were?

(SHELLEY shrugs, Who knows?)

SHELLEY. Mom never brought it up, but I'm pretty sure that if I'd confessed my affair with Tom, she would have told me I was adopted.

ELI. *(Admiringly.)* You made it up.

(SHELLEY turns her wheelchair to face ELI. He gives her a high-low-five.)

SHELLEY. *(Glances upstairs.)* It seems to have helped, anyway. Love doesn't seem to have a brain in its head, Eli, it can't add or subtract ….
ELI. Is that why it's the strongest force on earth?
SHELLEY. I wonder.

(Exeunt. The stage is empty.
In a moment the corroded muffler barks, explodes, and the truck is driven away. The rooster finally crows.
The bedroom door is opened cautiously. GEMMA, half-dressed, or robed, appears in the doorway. TOM stands behind her, half-loved, disheveled. They look around, listen.)

GEMMA. Have they gone?
TOM. *(Calls out.)* Anyone? *(After a moment.)* At last. I think we're alone.
GEMMA. I thought they'd never leave.
TOM. They'll be back.
GEMMA. Every one of them, but I don't mind.
TOM. No, not any more.
GEMMA. I missed you terribly.

(GEMMA leads him back into bedroom and closes the door behind them. As the curtain descends or the lights fade to black, a small squeal is heard from within.)

CURTAIN

ISBN 0 573 62870 X

#11111